(12456) P15

(4712) 6

D1799962

Ethnic Diversity and the Nation State

This book explores a largely forgotten legacy of multicultural political thought and practice from within Eastern Europe and examines its relevance to post-Cold War debates on state and nationhood. Featuring a Foreword by former UK Home Secretary Charles Clarke, it weaves theory and practice to challenge established understandings of the nation state.

Eastern Europe is still too often viewed through the prism of ethnic conflict, which overlooks the region's positive contribution to modern debates on the political management of ethno-cultural diversity, and towards the construction of a united Europe beyond the nation state. Based on extensive archival research in Estonia, Latvia, Germany, Russia, as well as the League of Nations Archive in Geneva, this book explores this neglected multicultural legacy and assesses its significance in the post-Cold War era, which has seen the reappearance of national cultural autonomy laws in several states of Eastern Europe.

Ethnic Diversity and the Nation State is invaluable reading for students and scholars of political science, history, sociology and European studies, and also for policymakers and others interested in minority rights and ethnic conflict regulation.

David J. Smith is Professor of History and Politics at the University of Glasgow, UK.

John Hiden is Emeritus Professor of European History, Bradford University, UK.

Routledge innovations in political theory

Ethnic Diversity and the Nation State

National cultural autonomy revisited

David J. Smith and John Hiden

Routledge
Taylor & Francis Group

LONDON AND NEW YORK

First published 2012
by Routledge
2 Park Square, Milton Park, Abingdon, Oxon OX14 4RN

Simultaneously published in the USA and Canada
by Routledge
711 Third Avenue, New York, NY 10017

Routledge is an imprint of the Taylor & Francis Group, an informa business

© 2012 David J. Smith and John Hiden

The right of David J. Smith and John Hiden to be identified as
authors of this work has been asserted by them in accordance
with sections 77 and 78 of the Copyright, Designs and Patents
Act 1988.

All rights reserved. No part of this book may be reprinted or
reproduced or utilized in any form or by any electronic,
mechanical, or other means, now known or hereafter
invented, including photocopying and recording, or in any
information storage or retrieval system, without permission in
writing from the publishers.

Trademark notice: Product or corporate names may be
trademarks or registered trademarks, and are used only for
identification and explanation without intent to infringe.

British Library Cataloguing in Publication Data
A catalogue record for this book is available from the British Library

Library of Congress Cataloging-in-Publication Data
Smith, David J. (David James), 1968–
Ethnic diversity and the nation state : national cultural
autonomy revisited / David J Smith and John Hiden.
    p. cm. – (Routledge innovations in political theory; 43)
    Includes bibliographical references and index.
    1. Europe, Eastern–Politics and government–1918–1945.
    2. Multiculturalism–Europe, Eastern–History. 3. Cultural
    pluralism–Europe, Eastern–History. 4. Minorities–Legal
    status, laws, etc.–Europe, Eastern–History. 5. Nation-state.
    6. Baltic States–Politics and government. 7. Congress of
    European Nationalities–History. I. Hiden, John. II. Title.
    JN96.A38M575 2012
    305.800947–dc23   2011047197

ISBN: 978-0-415-69690-6 (hbk)
ISBN: 978-0-203-11832-0 (ebk)

Typeset in Sabon
by Wearset Ltd, Boldon, Tyne and Wear

Printed and bound in Great Britain by
TJ International Ltd, Padstow, Cornwall

Contents

Foreword

One of the greatest political and social challenges of our times remains how to address nationalist feelings and sentiment in a way that does not result in violent and destructive conflict. In Europe today, the examples of the former Yugoslavia, the Basque country, Northern Ireland, Corsica and, in a rather different way, Belgium, Catalonia, Scotland and Wales all offer a reminder that nationalism remains a potent political force.

However, in the twentieth century the challenges were far greater. From 1848 onwards, nationalist feelings had expressed themselves powerfully, notably in the enormous Austro-Hungarian and Russian empires, where the nationalist aspiration was often progressive and forward-looking.

The immediate cause of the First World War was the assassination in 1914 in Sarajevo of Archduke Ferdinand by the Bosnian Serb nationalist Gavrilo Princip. The unsatisfactory Versailles settlement strengthened nationalist forces, notably in Germany, and led indirectly to the Second World War. And in its turn the Potsdam settlement legitimized the smothering Soviet blanket over central and Eastern Europe, which suppressed the many national identities that are now finding their expression after the collapse of the Soviet system.

Of course, throughout this period an enormous range of political thinkers and ideologists wrestled with the question of how to deal with nationalities. The traditional historic view was that nationality should be dealt with through the Western nation state principle which followed the model of countries like Britain, France, Germany, Italy, even the USA, where a traditional nation state had steadily evolved through an often difficult and bloody historical process that lasted centuries.

This thinking underlay the Versailles settlement, but really was difficult to apply in practice in the far more complicated inheritance of the Russian and Austro-Hungarian empires.

David Smith and John Hiden's exciting and interesting book looks at the ways in which this debate evolved both in theory and in practice. They focus particularly on the principle of non-territorial cultural autonomy or national cultural autonomy, which was first elaborated in depth by the Marxist social democratic political theorists Karl Renner (from 1899) and Otto Bauer (from 1907) who were very much informed by the experience of the Austro-Hungarian Empire.

Renner and Bauer regarded ethnicity and nationality as independent factors in social development, not simply as contingent on economic class. They therefore argued that any new political regime had to take account of national demands of different ethnic groups and minorities. They understood that the ambition for each nation to have their own state was not a practical aspiration in the complex ethnically mixed environment of central and eastern Europe without deep conflict and human suffering.

This outlook led directly to the need for procedures to protect ethnic minorities, which were instituted by the new League of Nations. However, these procedures were still founded in the traditional Western nation state model.

The national cultural autonomy approach of Renner and Bauer found little general application. The main exceptions during the 1920s were the newly established Baltic states of Estonia, Latvia and Lithuania. They had a striking willingness to embrace this new, idealistic but still comparatively novel and unproven approach. For example, in 1925 the Estonian government passed a law on the cultural autonomy of minorities, following which the Jewish Cultural Council was elected in 1926. This was disbanded only after the Soviet occupation of Estonia in 1940. This cultural autonomy allowed full control of education and so, from 1926, Hebrew began to replace Russian in the Jewish public school in Tallinn.

The global Jewish community saw the significance of cultural autonomy and so the Jewish National Endowment *Keren Kajamet* presented the Estonian government with a certificate of gratitude. In 1936, the *Jewish Chronicle* reported:

> Estonia is the only country in Eastern Europe where neither the Government nor the people practice any discrimination

against Jews and where Jews are left in peace ... the cultural autonomy granted to Estonian Jews ten years ago still holds good, and Jews are allowed to lead a free and unmolested life and fashion it in accord with their national and cultural principles.

The establishment of the European Nationalities Congress in 1925 sought to promote this approach and directly challenged the fixation with unitary, culturally homogenous nation states, which, for example, had been expressed by Joseph Stalin. His *Marxism and the National Question* in 1913 defined (at page 307) the nation as 'an historically formed, stable community of people, united by community of language, of territory, of economic life, and of psychological make-up, which expresses itself in community of culture'.

I found Smith and Hiden's focus on the Baltic experience of the 1920s particularly interesting. My wife's grandfather, August Maramaa, was a social democrat and the mayor of the Estonian town of Viljandi for most of the period between the two world wars where he sought to apply this philosophy. He was taken to Siberia in 1940 where he died – as did his wife and many of his family – victims of Stalin's approach to 'the nationality question'.

The detailed analysis offered by Smith and Hiden has a great deal to offer to modern policymakers trying to find practical solutions to these difficult and complex issues. Chapter 7 of the book sets out some of the ways in which these historic ideas resonate today.

As we look to the future within our globalized world in which individual identity is ever more important, it is the time to take forward the ideas of Renner and Bauer to modern times.

In recent decades the enormous movements of people, the process of economic and political change and the growth of a world media have significantly weakened the traditional nation state. Terrorism has raised people's fears to a new level and helped open the way to far-right, neo-fascist parties in Europe, all of them based on a backward-looking and inverted version of national identity.

I admire the work of Professor Amartya Sen, whose book *Identity and Violence* sets out a full analysis of the complex web of identities which each of us possesses. He starts from the obvious point that every individual has a vast range of identities, for example gender and sexuality, race, faith, parental background, profession/occupation, residency, age and so on. Nationality is one of the identities on this list, but only one.

From that it follows that each individual, *for themselves*, makes a choice between these identities and how much weight and priority to give them in their own lives. Everyone has to be able to make that choice freely for themselves and has the right not to be categorized in our whole lives by only one or perhaps two of our identities, for example predominantly by our nationality. It is not the case that everyone of a particular nationality has the same motivations; they do not.

Our political and social systems should accept that it is usual for people to have a range of identities, which include nationality, that individuals must be able to prioritize their own identities in accordance with their own lives and that no one should categorize you by just one of your identities alone.

I believe that these principles are the natural extension of the ideas of national cultural autonomy whose historical substance David Smith and John Hiden have charted so interestingly in this book. I am sure that it will help promote public understanding of the ways in which this approach could be given effect in the modern world.

Rt Hon. Charles Clarke

Preface

'One of the difficulties of the history of ideas is that names are more permanent than things. Institutions change, but the terms used to describe them remain the same.'[1] Alfred Cobban's words perfectly encapsulate the problem of writing about the nation state, a concept formed in the very specific conditions of late eighteenth-century Western Europe and North America. The nation state was classically defined in terms of congruence between a territorial state on the one hand and, on the other, a sovereign national community conceived as having a single homogeneous culture.

Few living within longer established European nation states, such as Britain and France, could meaningfully affirm these principles today in a world increasingly shaped by the processes of globalization. The notion of the unitary, indivisibly sovereign nation state has found itself challenged simultaneously from above by European integration and from below by the rise of regionalist movements. The migration of populations and its attendant intermingling of different peoples, meanwhile, has raised additional questions about how best to accommodate ethno-cultural diversity within existing state structures.

In seeking answers few would immediately think of looking towards central and Eastern Europe. All too often this region is viewed through the prism of the ethnic conflicts that defined it so markedly during the interwar period and which to some extent have been replicated after the fall of communism. Indeed, the whole thrust of post-communist 'transition' in central and Eastern Europe has been about imposing Western political and societal templates – paradoxically, at a time when such templates are themselves increasingly open to question and, therefore, redefinition.

Those policymakers seeking to graft Western European state models onto the region seem until recently to have been comparatively unaware of central and Eastern Europe's own positive contribution to modern debates on the political management of ethno-cultural diversity. They thus overlook the experiences and insights of an entire generation of political leaders who devoted their lives to the pursuit of realizing a democratic multicultural vision of nation and statehood based on the principle of shared territorial space. It was to explore this forgotten legacy that we devised and conducted the joint Arts and Humanities Research Council (AHRC)-funded research project, 'Ending nationalism? The quest for cultural autonomy in interwar Europe' (2003–2008, ref. 16232), on which this book is based.

At the centre of our investigation was the principle of non-territorial cultural autonomy, also referred to as national cultural autonomy (hereafter NCA or cultural autonomy). This concept was first elaborated in depth by the social democratic political theorists Karl Renner and Otto Bauer within the context of the late Austro-Hungarian Empire. Unlike earlier Marxist thinkers, Renner and Bauer did not view ethnicity and nationality as purely contingent on class-based economic relations, but as independent factors in social development. From this perspective, accommodation of the emerging national demands of subject ethnicities within the Empire was central to any proposed reform of the political order. The Austro-Marxists were, however, implacably opposed to the Western nation state principle then starting to gain currency within the Habsburg lands. They understood that in the complex ethnically mixed environment of central and Eastern Europe, the mantra 'for each nation a state' would be impossible to realize – impossible that is, without untold bloodshed and human suffering.

Renner and Bauer's point of departure therefore became the 'personal principle', which holds that 'totalities of persons are divisible only according to personal, not territorial characteristics'.[2] As part of a federalist political reform of the Empire, they argued, each national group should be given the opportunity to establish its own cultural self-government. The remit of this body would encompass the entire territory of the Habsburg state and would entail responsibility for organizing schooling in the relevant national language as well as other cultural matters specific to the nationality in question.

Cultural autonomy was piloted at a local level during the final years of the Habsburg Empire and also became highly influential within the neighbouring western regions of Tsarist Russia. War and revolution, however, soon brought about the complete collapse of these multinational states. Thereafter, Renner and Bauer's ideas were largely disregarded within the grand restructuring of European political space that took place during 1918–1923, paradoxically at a time when many millions of individuals fell into the category of national minority as a result of new states forming.

The minority protection procedures instituted by the new League of Nations acknowledged the difficulties of consolidating those new and enlarged states established under the peace settlement. However, these procedures were informed by Western state models, leaving little space for the implementation of the multinational vision of Renner and Bauer. The only exceptions were to be found in those new post-imperial states that were formed outwith the provisions of the Paris peace treaties. Foremost in taking up the thinking of Renner and Bauer during the 1920s were the newly established Baltic states of Estonia, Latvia and Lithuania. Their willingness to embrace a still comparatively novel and untested approach to state–society relations is striking.

It was for this reason that our research project focused heavily on the formative years of those three states and on Estonia and Latvia in particular. Their practical application of cultural autonomy inspired a debate that went far beyond the confines of the eastern Baltic region to the very heart of questions about the future of what was then optimistically termed the New Europe. While accepting the need to work within the new territorial boundaries established after the war, liberal national minority activists from the Baltic states nevertheless sought to look beyond the new nation state framework. Their work was critically important in bringing together like-minded individuals throughout Europe in a new transnational organization, the European Nationalities Congress, founded in the autumn of 1925. This initiative took the original ideas of Renner and Bauer and sought to adapt them to the new conditions of post-war Europe. In this way it directly challenged the fixation with unitary, indissolubly sovereign and culturally homogenous nation states – a concept contributing in large measure to the outbreak of a second generalized conflict in Europe only 20 years after the First World War had ended.

Telling the story of the 1920s European Nationalities Congress and the Baltic experiments that inspired it is both interesting and important from a purely historical standpoint, given the neglect in existing historiography of the liberal and multicultural heritage of central and Eastern Europe. Beyond this the interwar quest for cultural autonomy has a relevance to wholly contemporary European developments and debates. Since the fall of communism in central and Eastern Europe, new laws based on the principle of non-territorial cultural autonomy have been adopted or discussed in Hungary, Estonia, Russia, Romania and a range of other countries in the region. During the early stages of our own research in February 2005, we were invited to Bucharest to brief ministers, members of parliament and officials on Estonia's historic model of cultural autonomy, as part of discussions around the Romanian government's draft law on national minorities. This was part of a project conducted by the European Centre for Minority Issues in Flensburg, Germany and sponsored by the UK Foreign and Commonwealth Office.[3]

The Romanian visit gave rise to further joint academic–practitioner seminars on cultural autonomy during 2006–2007. The first of these took place in Glasgow in July 2006 and involved delegates from the Venice Commission of the Council of Europe, and the government of Romania. Additional funding from the AHRC pilot non-academic-user dissemination initiative enabled us to hold a round table, again in Glasgow, in January 2007. This included representatives of the Organization for Security and Co-operation in Europe (OSCE) and the governments of Hungary and Armenia. In May of the same year we organized a session on cultural autonomy ('The re-emergence of an old model') in Zagreb, Croatia, in conjunction with the Venice Commission, under the patronage of the President of Croatia and in cooperation with the country's Ministry of European Affairs and European Integration and the University of Zagreb. In his introductory address to the seminar, the Secretary of the Venice Commission, Gianni Buquicchio, stressed the value of assessing 'the real practical significance in modern Europe of this model'. While noting the particular relevance of cultural autonomy for the East European countries he also cited the application of the model in Belgium.[4] More generally, discussions at these seminars raised interesting further questions about the potential relevance of the ideas of Renner and Bauer for current debates on multiculturalism within Western Europe, North America and indeed the wider world.

Piecing together the quest for cultural autonomy in interwar Europe entailed prolonged periods of work in archives and libraries in Estonia, Latvia, Russia, Switzerland and Germany. Particular thanks are due to: all of the staff at the Estonian State Archive in Tallinn for their efficient and friendly assistance over several visits; Valters Ščerbinskis of the Latvian State Historical Archive, Riga; Bernhadine Pejovic of the League of Nations Archive, Geneva; Vladimir Korotaev and Nataliia Kolganova of the Russian State Historical Archive, Moscow; and Christopher and Elena Hill for their practical help and support during visits to Moscow. Peter Wörster of the Herder Institut, Marburg helped us to access additional items from the invaluable collection of private papers held there. He also first brought to our attention the fact that Ewald Ammende's personal papers from his early years are held at the Russian State Historical Archive in Moscow. Andreas Lawaty and Joachim Tauber not only gave us access to the excellent research library of the Nordost Institut in Lüneburg, but also provided us with a congenial writing space during several very enjoyable visits. Both have taken a keen interest in our project from the start and participated in the project seminar held in Glasgow during summer 2006.

We are pleased to acknowledge the financial support of the UK Arts and Humanities Research Council for this project, including the additional funds provided for the various joint academic–practitioner events towards the end. The Department of Central and East European Studies and, latterly, the UK Language-based Area Studies Centre for Russian and Central and East European Studies at the University of Glasgow also provided additional support towards travel and arranging project seminars.

Project seminars and other conferences attended during the course of the research provided us with valuable additional insights into our work. We are especially grateful to all who participated in the two joint academic–practitioner events held at the University of Glasgow in July 2006 and January 2007 and in the subsequent Universities for Democracy session co-organized with the Council of Europe Venice Commission in Zagreb in May 2007. Their comments, particularly those of two experts on liberal multiculturalism, Ephraim Nimni and Will Kymlicka, proved most helpful. Thanks also to Karl Cordell for helping to arrange and later co-editing the publication that arose from the 2006 joint seminar, first in the form of a special issue of *Ethnopolitics* and later as an edited volume.

Panels outlining aspects of the research were also organized at the annual convention of the Association for the Study of Nationalities (2004) and the five-yearly World Congress of the International Committee for Central and East European Studies (2005). In addition, papers were delivered at conferences and symposia in Glasgow, Belfast, Klaipeda, London and Tartu, as well as at the Roundtable Conference on Cultural Autonomy in February 2008 in Shrivenham, co-hosted by the Defence Academy of the United Kingdom and the New Security Foundation. Of the many colleagues with whom we have worked during the project, we would particularly like to acknowledge the value of our discussions with Martyn Housden of the University of Bradford, Leonidas Donskis of Vytautas Magnus University, and Vytautas Petronis, who held an ESRC Postdoctoral Fellowship at the University of Glasgow during 2009–2010 and is at the time of writing a Fellow at the Herder Institut, Marburg.

Researching and writing this book has entailed frequent periods of absence from home over several years. David Smith wishes to thank his wife Sanna and daughter Anni for their support and forbearance during this time. John Hiden, as always, has drawn on the selfless support and good company of his wife, Juliet.

David Smith and John Hiden
1 November 2011

1 Nation, state and minority in modern Europe

The concept of national minority is inextricably linked to the emergence of the modern state and the rise of nationalism as an ideology and political movement. All collective national identities are based to varying degrees on ethno-cultural as well as civic components and the modern nation state project has typically aspired to make national space congruent with political space.[1] This in turn has held implications for the status of those residents whose cultural characteristics mark them out as distinct from the dominant ethno-cultural core within the state.[2]

In the western part of Europe, unitary centralized states were already taking shape prior to the age of nationalism. Over a long period of time these states ironed out many of the pre-existing ethnic and regional differences amongst their populations and moulded relatively coherent national identities, rooted in shared institutions and a single official language of administration, education and social communication.[3] Within this context, the term 'minority' became applicable mainly to new migrant populations, while minority rights were treated as a matter of ensuring freedom from discrimination on ethnic grounds.[4] That new immigrant minorities would assimilate into the 'common core' or dominant societal culture was taken as read.

The Western European model of state- and nation-building has, however, undergone significant change during recent decades. Greater tolerance and recognition of cultural diversity are now acknowledged as important building blocks in the construction of integrated political communities. This understanding has involved, *inter alia*, according varying degrees of public recognition to the distinct cultures of migrant groups.[5] Numerous well-established Western democracies have also had to contend with new or resurgent movements in the name of more historically rooted minority groups laying claim to sovereignty over particular territorial sub-regions of the state. As a result many governments have made moves in the direction of territorial devolution and the recognition of minority languages. Thus, after having once deemed ethnicity as irrelevant, Western liberal democracies have found themselves confronted with the 'dilemma of ethno-cultural diversity' – how to ensure equal treatment and adequate cultural recognition for different ethnicities without undermining societal cohesion.[6]

In central and Eastern Europe, by contrast, with its long history of mixed settlement, the political management of multiculturalism has been a central preoccupation from the very outset of the modern state-building process. Here, nationalism as an ideology and political movement took hold within the context of empire. Driven by disaffected new intellectual strata amongst the subject peoples, it was grounded in identification with an ethnic community rather than with established political institutions.[7] The nationalist programme was, therefore, concerned not only with achieving civic equality, but also with maintaining the cultural distinctiveness of one's particular group, often in the face of growing efforts to erode that identity from above. In the case of larger, more compactly settled populations, nationalist demands were soon linked to particular territories, which, however imprecisely defined, were deemed to be the national homeland of the group in question. This territorial frame of reference would later become central to the new political order arising from the rapid and largely unanticipated collapse of the central and East European empires during 1914–1923.

The Bolshevik regime that took power in Russia from 1917 was quite prepared to crush separatist national movements in the name of proletarian solidarity. Nevertheless, Bolshevik leaders had already realized that they would also need to accord at least some recognition to prior demands for national self-determination if communism was to consolidate its hold over much of the former Tsarist Empire. In keeping with Josef Stalin's 1913 definition of nation as a territorially based community, the new Soviet state was structured along ethno-territorial lines.[8] In the process, the new government was trying at the same time to underscore a symbolic break with the Great Russian chauvinism of the Tsarist past. This territorial approach went some way towards accommodating demands for self-determination made on behalf of larger more compactly settled national groups. It did not, however, cater for more dispersed communities, most notably the Jews.

The new Union of Soviet Socialist Republics (USSR) established in 1922 also fell far short of being a genuinely democratic multinational federation. While the federal structure ultimately endured throughout the entire seven decades of Soviet power, it was not necessarily understood by its creators as anything other than a transitional expedient in the construction of a transcendent Soviet identity. The dictum 'national in form, socialist [read Soviet] in content' betrayed an agenda in which the expression of cultural pluralism was strictly subordinated to the goal of maintaining tight centralized control by a single party. This state of affairs intensified once Stalin had consolidated his power base in the late 1920s. Autonomous-minded party elites in the various national republics were purged in the course of the 1930s, while the leading role of the Russian people within the Soviet state was increasingly underlined within official discourse. All such trends were amplified by the onset of war in 1941, which went hand in hand with the forcible resettlement of entire ethnic groups by the Soviet authorities.

Despite a reversion to the Leninist policies of cultural pluralism during the post-Stalin era, the Soviet state was never able to resolve the basic contradictions at the heart of its nationalities policy, which has been aptly described as formed by an 'affirmative action empire' and a system of 'federal colonialism'.[9] By linking enjoyment of national rights strictly to territory while simultaneously assigning a personal ethno-national identity to each individual citizen, the Soviet state institutionalized a tension that has had profound consequences for nation-building in the successor states to the USSR.[10]

Further westward, the successor states established in the territories between Germany and Soviet Russia after the First World War were explicitly understood as the states of and for particular ethnic nations. In all cases, however, a significant part of the population belonged to a different ethnic category. These non-titular ethnicities had for the most part already established a separate societal culture prior to the collapse of empire. Some had formerly constituted the ruling elite within the territories in question; others had articulated their own demands for cultural recognition and/or territorial sovereignty.[11] Under these circumstances, one could hardly assume a smooth process of voluntary assimilation into the majority culture of the new countries of residence. De facto, therefore, the new countries of central Europe were 'plural society states' whose consolidation would require 'reaction to diverse political and national demands'.[12]

The victorious Western Powers acknowledged this reality by insisting that the states created or enlarged under the terms of the post-war peace settlement sign minority rights treaties. These stipulated that persons belonging to national minorities should enjoy equal rights as citizens in addition to certain guarantees relating to the practice of their distinct culture, such as the right to basic state-funded education in their mother tongue. Any infringements of the treaties were to be reported to the newly created League of Nations, which devised an elaborate system of petitions for minority complaints. Sadly, the League, never stronger than the sum of its parts, was ultimately ill-placed to counter the continued allure of nationalism within post-war Europe, which became irresistible following the onset of the Great Depression and Hitler's rise to power in Germany. The subsequent events of 1933–1945 – not least the manipulation of the minority question by Nazi Germany in the run-up to war – led many observers to conclude that collective minority rights had been part of the problem, rather than a solution. Far from regulating ethnic tensions, it was argued, such rights had merely contributed to growing instability and irredentist sentiment within the new states of central Europe.[13]

The League model of collective minority rights thus found itself widely discredited in the wake of the Second World War. For all of the ravages wrought by mass murder, forced population transfers and border changes during 1939–1948, national and political space were still far from congruent in post-war central and Eastern Europe. Yet the Soviet-sponsored, state socialist regimes that took power in the region were largely ill-disposed to grant cultural recognition to minority groups living within their borders.[14] More generally, the concept of collective minority rights all but disappeared from international legal discourse. Instead, the post-war agreements drawn up under the auspices of the United Nations, Council of Europe and Conference for Security and Cooperation in Europe saw minority rights as a matter of guaranteeing individual human rights – no specific collective provisions were envisaged.[15]

To view interwar central and Eastern Europe largely through the prism of 1933–1945 is, however, to neglect the more positive trends apparent within the region during the 1920s. Here, the work of the Congress of European Nationalities (also popularly known as the Nationalities Congress, and hereinafter referred to as such), a transnational lobby group formed in 1925, offers a case in point. The few existing studies of the Congress to date, most notably Sabine Bamberger-Stemmann's exhaustive survey published in 2000, have taken their cue from the 1930s when the Nazi government in Germany was able to extend its influence over the German minority representatives from various countries that had always formed the core of the Congress. In light of this it has often been assumed that from its very inception the Congress was little more than a cover for efforts by Germany to revise the territorial provisions of the post-First World War peace settlement.[16]

This interpretation fundamentally misrepresents what the Congress was about during the first five or six years of its existence, when the organization was headed by a quite remarkable group of liberal minority rights activists – both German and non-German – from across central and Eastern Europe. The ideas that they aired during this period often appear startlingly relevant to present-day debates on European integration and in tune with the preoccupations of postmodern political theorists.[17] Encompassing representatives speaking in the name of 34 national minorities from 18 European states, the Congress sought mainly to effect a change to the League of Nations minority procedures. While Congress leaders welcomed the protection afforded by the League against the threat of dissimilation, they considered the system deficient when it came to ensuring the long-term preservation of minority languages and cultures.

Indeed, when considering central and Eastern Europe, League representatives signalled their clear commitment to building indivisibly sovereign, one-community nation states on the Western European model. Any suggestion of creating autonomous national minority institutions as an intermediary between state and individual was seen as conducive to creating states within states and fuelling irredentism. The more limited, individually based rights adopted by the League were thus seen as little more than a temporary expedient, which would prepare national minorities for eventual merger into the dominant societal culture of the state in which they lived.[18]

While acknowledging the need to work within the territorial frontiers established in 1919–1923, the founding fathers of the Nationalities Congress nevertheless saw the one-community nation state model as fundamentally ill-suited to the ethnically complex environment of central and Eastern Europe. With different ethnicities thoroughly intermingled, any attempt to assert exclusive ownership by a particular group over territory would necessarily generate huge discontent. The only solution was to move towards an understanding of the state as a shared territorial space occupied by different ethnic groups, all of which had a fundamental interest in the welfare of their common homeland. In keeping with this, Congress leaders conceived of the cultural nation (*Kulturnation*) as a collectivity of persons, voluntarily united in the form of a corporation at public law. Such public–legal status would act as a foundation for the establishment of cultural self-governments. These would have jurisdiction over native-language schooling across the territory of the given state, as well as dealing with cultural matters of specific concern to the minority community.

Another key demand of the Congress was the establishment of a permanent minority commission at the League of Nations in order to give organized national minorities an international public–legal status comparable to that enjoyed by representatives of states. In the longer term, the goal was to bring about the formation of a federalist Europe transcending the narrow particularism of the nation state; in other words a genuine 'Europe of peoples'.

The Congress leaders of the 1920s were inspired by the ideas of Karl Renner and Otto Bauer, as well as by other pioneers of multicultural state- and nation-building within the late nineteenth and early twentieth-century empires of central and Eastern Europe. Other key influences, however, were the unique experiments with non-territorial cultural autonomy being pursued after the First World War in the newly established Baltic states of Estonia, Latvia and Lithuania. Of the leading members of the Congress during the late 1920s, two – Ewald Ammende and Paul Schiemann – were Baltic Germans from Estonia and Latvia respectively. A third, the ethnic Russian Mikhail Kurchinskii, also hailed from Estonia. It is no coincidence, therefore, that the first meeting of the Nationalities Congress took place shortly after the adoption of Estonia's celebrated 1925 law on cultural autonomy for national minorities. Discussions of similar legislation were still ongoing in Latvia, although it had already afforded broad autonomy to its national minorities under a schooling law of 1919.

In recent years, a number of biographical studies of Congress leaders have explored the links between their activities at the international level and the formative environments within which their ideas came to fruition.[19] The only substantial existing study of the Nationalities Congress, however, focuses chiefly on issues of organization and on the nature of links with Germany rather than on the ideal of cultural autonomy that stimulated such rich and diverse debates during the late 1920s.[20]

There are a number of accounts of the unique cultural autonomy laws adopted in the interwar Baltic states, and the biggest body of literature relates to the Estonian legislation of 1925.[21] The corresponding laws in Latvia and Lithuania have received comparatively less attention.[22] Other authors allude to autonomy within the context of a broader consideration of the experiences of individual minority groups living within these countries.[23] On the whole, these existing works focus on the origins of cultural autonomy rather than the actual, practical implementation of laws and the day-to-day running of institutions set up for this purpose. This remains the case even for the path-breaking cultural autonomy legislation adopted in Estonia after 1925.[24]

The present work redresses the balance by providing a comparative analysis of the origins, theory and practice of cultural autonomy in all three Baltic states during the interwar period, as well as examining in this context the varying German, Jewish and Russian experiences of autonomous institutions. In addition, the study locates the Baltic case within its wider international setting, still too often neglected in general books about these countries. Our work especially emphasizes the interlinkages between the politics and practice of autonomy in the Baltic countries and the work of the Nationalities Congress, drawing on materials collected from state archives in Estonia, Latvia and the Russian Federation, as well as the League of Nations Archive in Geneva. Use has also been made of the substantial collections at the Johann Gottfried Herder Institut in Marburg, the Nordost Institut in Lüneburg and the National Libraries of Latvia and Estonia, both of which house important newspaper archives.

To reiterate the point we made in the Preface, a study of this kind is intrinsically interesting from a historical point of view, opening up a wholly new perspective on minority issues in interwar central and Eastern Europe. Yet it also resonates with developments in the region following the collapse of communism and the demise of the USSR, when with the end of the Cold War, the 'dilemma of ethno-cultural diversity' and the issue of targeted minority rights were thrust dramatically back onto the European agenda.

2 Voices in the wilderness?

Nationality issues were highlighted as never before during the 20 years leading up to the First World War. This was particularly so in the multi-ethnic empires of central and Eastern Europe, which lacked the relative cultural homogeneity and centralized government characteristic of Western states. Moreover, whatever attempts the empires made to appropriate the features of modern statehood were by this time certain to run up against the growing national consciousness of their subject peoples. One of the clearest indications of this was the outbreak of revolution in Russia in 1905, which catalysed demands for recognition of distinct ethnocultural nationality amongst the Tsarist Empire's minority groups.

Significantly, these demands were for autonomy rather than outright independence and that remained the case when the national question again came to the fore in the aftermath of Russia's February 1917 Revolution. There was thus anything but an inexorable progression from poly-ethnic empire towards independent nation-statehood during the approach to war in 1914.[1] It would be truer to say that the subject peoples, or some of them at least, had nation-statehood thrust upon them as a result of the sudden collapse of the dynasties under the pressures of war and revolution. The process was consolidated by the bias of the peace settlement towards the purely territorial expression of national identity.

The central place given to the nation state within the post-1918 international order has reinforced the perception of separatist nationalism as the dominant political trend within the pre-First World War empires. By extension, it has also obscured the many novel attempts that were made to promote a democratic and multinational vision of statehood within the existing borders of empire. Yet these efforts cannot be dismissed as mere voices in the wilderness. The ideas did not simply vanish in the smoke of battle, but persisted well into the interwar years and provided a foundation for innovative approaches to issues of nationality and territoriality.

These initiatives were informed first and foremost by the work of the Austrian social democrats Karl Renner and Otto Bauer during the last years of the Habsburg Empire. By the mid-1890s, the socialist movement in the Austrian half of the dual monarchy faced a growing challenge from radical nationalist parties seeking to ferment division between workers from different ethnic backgrounds. The national question thus became a matter of everyday practical politics from which no Austrian social democrat could remain aloof. The Social Democratic Party responded by reconstituting itself along multinational lines in 1897 and advocating the transformation of the Empire into a genuinely democratic federation of peoples.[2]

As the key thinkers of Austrian social democracy, Renner and Bauer vigorously attacked the essentialist, 'petty bourgeois' claim that nations and ethnic groups were natural and primordial entities with their own unique spirit. At the same time, they dismissed the 'naive cosmopolitanism' of orthodox Marxists, who saw national identity as entirely contingent on capitalism and thus inexorably set to disappear once a socialist order had been achieved.[3] For Renner and Bauer, nations were substantive historical and social constructs, 'communities of character' born out of constant reciprocal interaction between those subject to a common cultural influence and sharing a common language.[4] While nationhood could rest upon shared descent, this was by no means preordained. The national 'community of culture', Bauer observed in 1907, is 'never solely a community of nature' – the character of particular individuals is also determined by the culture and customs handed down to them, the education they receive, the laws to which they are subject and the manner in which they acquire their livelihood. In this respect, continued Bauer, 'the conscious choice of membership of a nation other than that of one's birth is possible', as is belonging to an equal or almost equal degree in the cultures of two or more nations.[5]

In formulating their ideas, Renner and Bauer followed Karl Kautsky's maxim that socialists had to be against all repression, including national.[6] One effect of capitalism, they argued, had been to divide pre-existing ethno-linguistic communities according to education and rights to political participation. The task of socialism was thus to draw 'the people as a whole' into the relevant (ethno) national community through democratization of cultural and political life.[7] In the particular context of the Habsburg Empire, emerging class divisions under capitalism had also followed ethnic lines, with German, Hungarian, Polish and Italian ruling strata presiding over largely Slavic 'subject peoples' such as the Czechs, Ruthenians, Slovaks and Slovenes. From the mid-nineteenth century onwards, emerging intellectual and bourgeois strata drawn from these so-called non-historic nations had begun to question their condition of cultural and political subordination. The nature of the Austrian Constitution, however, meant that those seeking greater national rights had little option but to try to capture power at the state level, as this provided the only mechanism for ensuring proper recognition of one's culture.[8] The political logic thus became one of organization along national lines and competition for power between different groups. It was this state of affairs above all that pitted workers of different ethnicities against one another and in doing so risked diverting attention away from the class struggle. Renner and Bauer quickly realized, therefore, that it would be impossible to advance the socialist agenda without redrawing the existing Habsburg state into a genuinely democratic federation of nationalities. As Bauer put it:

> the power of the nations to satisfy their cultural needs must be legally guaranteed if the population is no longer to be forced to divide into national parties, if conflict between national groups is not to make the class struggle impossible.[9]

While various proposals for the territorial federalization of Austria had been floated since 1848, the complex ethnic composition of the Empire – constantly shifting due to internal migration – made it difficult to conceive of a solution solely on this basis: however one drew the boundaries, each legally demarcated national region would inevitably contain national minorities, thereby simply replicating the existing problems of the Empire in miniature. The solution was, therefore, to separate the idea of the nation from that of territory and to allocate national rights according to what Renner termed 'the personality principle'. This aimed to:

constitute the nation not as a territorial corporation, but as an association of persons. The national bodies regulated by public law would thus constitute territorial bodies only insofar as their efficacy could not extend, of course, beyond the borders of the empire. Within the state, however, power would not be given to the Germans in one region and the Czechs in another; rather, each nation, wherever its members resided, would form a body that independently administered its own affairs.[10]

The personality principle was advocated by the south Slav delegation at the first all-Austrian Social Democratic Party Congress (*Gesamtparteitag*) held in Brünn (Brno) in September 1899 and found its way into the final Congress resolution outlining the steps necessary to achieve a national peace.[11] Renner elaborated the principle more fully through his pamphlet 'State and Nation', published that same year, in which he envisaged the nation as a public law corporation, in a position comparable to that of the Church. Just as the latter embraced communities of shared belief, so the nation should be thought of as an association of equal individuals, bound by a common culture.[12]

Personal choice was absolutely central to Renner's view of how nationality is determined. As he put it, 'the declared will of the person, the juridical and the natural, is the soul of legal existence'.[13] Nevertheless, the extent of this free will had to be determined with reference to the interests of the state as a whole. Thus, when Renner allocated to the national group responsibility for managing its own culture and schooling, he envisaged that this would fall within a basic legal framework prescribed by the state. His use of the term 'state free' in this context was, therefore, a qualified one, which highlighted by contrast those areas seen as the preserve of the state alone. Most obviously, these included the economy, military power, justice and policing.[14]

A subsequent work by Renner, *The Struggle of the Austrian Nations for the State* (1902), drew up a detailed blueprint for a multinational federal Austria. Territorially, the state was to be divided into cantons, each with its own elected council. Where cantons were nationally homogeneous the council would be responsible for all aspects of public administration, including schooling and other cultural functions. In nationally mixed cantons (in practice the vast majority) the elected council would be supplemented by two or more bodies of national self-administration, constituted on the basis of individual citizens freely entering their names onto a national register. These national delegations, as Renner called them, would have the power to levy taxes from those listed on the register and would deal independently with cultural tasks (primarily education) pertaining to the relevant ethnic group. The canton council, meanwhile, would be responsible solely for administrative tasks of a 'nationally neutral' character.[15]

At a higher administrative level, each *Land* or province of the state would have its own assembly, appointed by the cantons; these would deal with matters of common concern to all citizens. Operating in parallel to these assemblies would be *Land* national councils elected jointly by the local national delegations and the nationally homogeneous cantons, with responsibility for the cultural affairs of the relevant nationality. These dual administrative structures were to be further replicated at the overall state level, where national councils would take responsibility for higher education of the various nationalities.

In nationally homogeneous cantons, public administration was to be conducted in the language of the local majority; in those that were ethnically mixed, each national delegation would conduct its affairs in its own language, while the canton council and its areas of administrative responsibility would operate on a bi- or multilingual basis.[16] In essence, Renner set out to:

> cut in two the sum of the activities of the state, separating national and political matters. We must organize the population twice; once along the lines of nationality, the second time in relation to the state, and each time in administrative units of different form.[17]

If this could be achieved, he reasoned, national disputes would no longer impede 'the advance of the classes'. Under the proposed system, the classes of a single nation would confront each other within the canton councils of nationally homogenous territories and within the various delegations of the nationally mixed ones. Different nations would come together within the councils of the mixed cantons and *Länder* and within the representative assembly of the state as a whole. In so far as these bodies had no power to rule on national affairs, however, 'they could give the nations nothing and take nothing from them; here too the population would be organized according to classes, not according to nations'.[18]

Renner's scheme rested on the presumption that the withdrawal of the state from the sphere of culture would pave the way to national peace, just as its earlier withdrawal from the sphere of religion had settled confessional disputes.[19] Just as religious belief did not necessarily affect an individual's rights and responsibilities as a citizen, so it was believed that different ethnic groups could coexist harmoniously for the overall good of the state in which they lived. According to Bauer, the existing 'centralist-atomist' model of the state made 'the aspiration to national conquests [i.e. assimilation of other ethnicities] … the law of all national struggle'. While assimilation would still occur in a state organized according to the personality principle, it would derive from economic and 'convivial' relationships between different ethnicities and the 'natural force of attraction' of particular cultures, rather than the 'brutal force of a law that denies people of one nation the means of maintaining a cultural community with their fellow nationals'.[20]

In saying this, Renner and Bauer recognized that personal cultural autonomy could not wholly eradicate the wellsprings of nationalist contention where there remained socio-economic disparities between different groups. In a situation where, say, German enterprise owners benefited from the surplus value of Czech labour, the fiscal capacity of the Czech workers to develop national-cultural self-government would necessarily be limited. Any proposal to remedy this state of affairs through redistributive taxation, however, could easily become the object of nationalist quarrels within the relevant canton or *Land* council. As Bauer saw it, such a prospect would always remain open as long as the capitalist socio-economic order persisted.[21]

In other respects, too, Renner and Bauer's scheme raises interesting questions concerning the boundaries between culture and politics. How, for instance, does a state based on personal autonomy ensure communication and interaction across institutionalized ethnic boundaries and the construction of a shared civic space and identity embracing all residents? Bauer's work from 1907 implies that such interaction would occur as a matter of course in the economic sphere provided that the economy was not structured along national-territorial lines; perhaps more questionably, Bauer maintained that the more the working masses were exposed to education within their particular national-cultural context, the more internationalist they would become in their outlook. Also, as already noted, the system of nationally based education did not imply a complete absence of state regulation, which could be used to instil a common overarching civic identity.

There remains, however, the question of how to ensure that institutionalization of boundaries does not become an end in itself. A recent critique of national-cultural autonomy observes that 'once one assigns strong moral value to the intergenerational continuity of particular national cultures, it follows almost inevitably that fluid and overlapping boundaries between nations will be regarded as an irregularity that undermines the value of national membership'.[22] In this regard, Bauer's vision of different cultures competing peacefully for the affiliation of individual citizens appears somewhat fanciful, since national elites will have an instrumental interest in maximizing the numbers of those belonging to the particular group and, in this way, sustaining the institutional basis for cultural autonomy. As we shall see, these were issues that had to be confronted in practice in the interwar Baltic states where fully-fledged schemes of cultural autonomy were subsequently introduced.

In the more immediate term, Renner and Bauer's ideas were highly significant in shaping discussions on the nationality question in late-imperial Austria.[23] The personality principle was soon tested in practice in the form of the so-called Moravian Compromise of 1905. The arrangement involved drawing up national registers or cadastres on the basis of individual self-declaration in an effort to resolve Czech–German nationalist disputes over control of schooling and local government. By the eve of the First World War similar compromises were on the point of being implemented in the Bohemian town of Budweis (Budvar) and the Galician region of Austria.[24] As Bauer himself observed, the Moravian Compromise was not about instituting cultural autonomy in the sense intended by Renner: the registers that were established were used to elect national curia within a single provincial assembly, as part of a centralist-atomist constitutional arrangement still geared to competition between nationally based parties. In spite of this, Bauer still felt able to declare that:

> the first legislative attempt to base a new form of regulating the public right of nations on the personality principle is

without doubt an auspicious beginning, a clear sign that the conviction is growing that national relations in Austria cannot be regulated purely on the basis of the territorial principle – the first victory of a [genuine] principle.[25]

Renner and Bauer's 'organic-federal' conception of statehood also struck a chord within the neighbouring Tsarist Russian Empire where similar ideas were taking root at the turn of the twentieth century. Here, too, the inequality and repression endured by many nationalities were seen as a potent barrier to the realization of social and political freedom for the individual. Most obviously, non-territorial cultural autonomy had relevance for the unassimilated and geographically dispersed Jewish communities of Russia's western borderlands. Austro-Marxist thinking was espoused first by the socialist *Bund* and later (as a concept of diaspora rights) by the Zionists and the *Folkspartei*.[26]

Those speaking in the name of other, more compactly settled nationalities, such as the Estonians, Latvians and Lithuanians, had already begun to call for a territorial form of autonomy based on an identifiable ethnic homeland.[27] Yet even these groups were aware of the value of cultural autonomy as an adjunct to any territorial redrawing of the Empire. As late as September 1917, after the Russian provisional government had consented to a new province of Estland within ethnographic boundaries, key representatives of the Estonian national movement, such as Karl Ast, Ado Birk, Ardo Jürgenstein and Otto Strandman, continued to discuss the ideas of Renner and Bauer with which all had become familiar in the course of the preceding decade.[28]

Despite the obvious importance of Habsburg developments for those living in Russia, the traffic was not entirely one way. The ideas of Karl Renner bore a striking resemblance to those developed simultaneously yet separately by the Litvak historian, politician and leading minority rights theorist Simon Dubnow in his *Letters on Old and New Jewry* (published 1897–1907).[29] Unlike the members of the *Bund*, Dubnow and his followers were not opposed to the project of creating a Jewish national state in Palestine. At the same time they foresaw the continued existence of a Jewish diaspora that would need to be provided for within its states of residence. Drawing on long-standing traditions of Litvak autonomy within the Polish Commonwealth, Dubnow proposed non-territorial cultural autonomy as a model that would enable the Jewish communities of Europe to maintain their distinct identity and their own languages (Yiddish and Hebrew). At the same time, in Dubnow's view, Jews should enjoy equal rights within their host societies and pursue integration with the majority societal culture by attaining a good command of the official state language(s). His ideas were central to the programme of the *Soyuz Polnopraviia* (Committee for the Protection of Emancipation of Russian Jews) formed in Vilnius during the revolution of 1905.[30]

The upheavals of that year reflected a more generalized groundswell of demands for autonomy amongst the non-Russian nationalities of the Empire, including the Estonians, Latvians and Lithuanians.[31] The process could hardly leave untouched the traditional supremacy of the Baltic Germans, who for centuries had held sway over the provinces of Estland, Livland and Courland. The German elites had enjoyed extensive autonomy under a succession of rulers, most recently the Tsar, giving them complete political and social ascendancy over the region's peasantry. Since the machinery of government was monopolized by the landed nobility, and German was the language of administration and education, any social advance for the local peasantry had to be through Germanization. From the last quarter of the nineteenth century, however, the German elites faced a two-pronged challenge. From below came the Estonian and Latvian national awakenings, while from above the Tsarist state intensified policies of Russification geared towards greater administrative and, increasingly, cultural standardization.[32]

The precarious situation of the Baltic German nobility was graphically underlined by the violence visited upon them by the local peasantry during the revolution of 1905. From here on, most within the Baltic German community increasingly saw themselves as part of an embattled national minority rather than a privileged ruling caste. While the landed nobility did recover many of the formal trappings of power once the Tsarist government had restored order, the bitter experiences of 1905 hastened the formation for the first time of Baltic German associations (*Vereine*) spanning all three provinces. These focused above all on safeguarding German schooling and culture against any renewed challenges from the Russian government. Significantly, therefore, the *Vereine* marked an important shift towards closer cooperation between the ruling landed elites and the urban German bourgeoisie.[33] In short, the Renner and Bauer model of cultural autonomy, as opposed to simply defence of historic rights, could now be seen to have relevance to the Baltic Germans too.

A few enlightened souls amongst the Baltic Germans, notably the prominent journalist and commentator Paul Schiemann, responded by urging collaboration with Estonians and Latvians and political reform, which would allow the latter into government. Indeed the *Baltische Konstitutionelle Partei* that Schiemann and others were instrumental in establishing explicitly sought to broaden its membership beyond the Baltic German community, if without very much success.[34] Clearly, the rigidity of the social order and the accumulated bitterness of the Estonian and Latvian national leaders against the historic German overlords ruled out any possibility of a united front in defence of national rights.

More generally, the ideas of Renner and Bauer had little time to take root before war and revolution brought about the collapse of the European empires. In the Habsburg lands, many Czech national leaders had not been won over to the concept of shared territorial space, continuing to press for the nationalization of Bohemia and Moravia along Czech lines. In their view, forming national registers on the basis of free affiliation would perpetuate German cultural predominance by making it easier for people of Czech origin to send their children to German-language schools. The social democratic *Gesamtpartei* that Renner and Bauer had worked so hard to keep together had also unravelled along national lines by 1911.[35] Nevertheless, due weight must be given to the attempts to reconcile national differences on the basis of the personality principle. These were after all completely novel and it took the outbreak of a European-wide conflict to derail them completely.[36]

In the neighbouring Tsarist Russian Empire, the February 1917 Revolution was the event which opened up space for those political forces already attracted to Renner and Bauer's thinking. The onset of democratization, however, proved to be an all too brief interlude, as the events of October 1917 paved the way to Bolshevik control over most of the territory formerly ruled by the Romanovs. On paper, the new Union of Soviet Socialist Republics (USSR) formed in 1922 was a multinational federal state. In practice, Bolshevik nationalities policy improvised during the course of the Revolution proved thoroughly inimical to the ideas of the Austro-Marxists. First and foremost, the Soviet regime was wholly undemocratic. Its claim to uphold cultural pluralism was in practice integral to its drive to consolidate a single-party dictatorship, according to the doctrine of 'national in form, socialist in content'. Paul Schiemann, ever an astute observer of the region's politics, would later cynically react to Soviet pretensions to uphold cultural autonomy with the comment that Germans living in the Soviet Union were permitted to read Marx but not Goethe.[37]

Soviet thinking, moreover, took its cue from Josef Stalin's 1913 tract, 'Marxism and the National Question'. This defined nation as 'a historically constituted, stable community of people, formed on the basis of a common language, territory, economic life, and psychological make-up manifested in a common culture'.[38] Those national rights that did exist within the USSR were, therefore, conferred on a strictly territorial basis which made no provision for the needs of smaller, more dispersed groups or those who happened to be residing outside a designated ethnic homeland. Furthermore, the Soviet model lacked any element of personal choice: nationality was viewed as a primordial category conferred by birth. The only exceptions in this regard were those born to parents of different ethnicities, who were permitted to determine their own affiliation upon coming of age.

In the areas once controlled by the Habsburg, Hohenzollern and Ottoman dynasties and in those former western border regions that broke away from Russia after 1917, the territorial principle also held sway when it came to matters of national self-determination. The new, independent successor states that emerged from the empires were for the most part created in the name of single titular ethnic groups, even though all contained a variety of different ethnicities, each with its own national awareness. The danger was that the new states would engage in 'nationalizing' policies that prioritized the needs of the majority people at the expense of new national minorities living within their borders. This seemed most likely in those cases where a minority had formerly constituted part of the ruling elite within the old empire, and could thus be portrayed as responsible for past injustices visited upon the new state-bearing nation prior to independence.

Such an approach raised the spectre of a backlash on the part of national minorities. In those cases – such as the German and the Hungarian – where representatives of a minority nationality could look externally to 'a nation-state of their own', any perceived injustices might encourage this 'external national home-land' to champion the rights of its ethno-national kinfolk abroad, in effect assuming the role of protector of the entire *Volk* rather than simply its own citizens.[39]

Indeed, *völkisch*-nationalist commentators in Germany made no secret of their desire to transform the Reich German state consciousness into pan-German national awareness. One such writer, influential in right-wing circles, was Max Hildebert-Boehm, originally from the Baltic provinces of Russia. In his provocative book, *Europa Irredenta*, published in 1923, Boehm appeared to deny small states any right to existence: 'The dependence of the small on the large,' he wrote, 'is a fundamental in the lives of individuals and peoples, whose brutality can be modified and its form changed, but which in essence is inescapable.' Of the peace settlement he went on to say: 'The mutilation of Europe has altered the function of its members in anarchic arbitrariness. Big nations are artificially restrained, medium states blown up to great powers. This situation will not last.'[40]

The victorious Allied Powers showed their awareness of the potential danger of ethnic conflict by insisting that those successor states created by the peace settlement after the First World War sign treaties for the protection of national minorities. The prototype for these treaties was the agreement signed by Poland in 1919. Under its terms, persons belonging to national minorities were promised equal rights as citizens, as well as certain specific rights pertaining to the preservation and practice of their distinct culture. These included the right to native-language primary schooling for all citizens in addition to the right to set up private associations for cultural purposes. Any infringements of the treaties could be reported to the newly established League of Nations. In that respect, the nationalities question was at last internationalized, thus raising hopes that new European-wide statute law on minority rights would eventually be enacted.[41] Such a prospect, however, receded into the distance as minority activists quickly became disillusioned with the laborious appeals procedures created by the League of Nations.

Redress for perceived violations of the minority protection clauses in the treaties had to be sought initially by sending a petition to the Minorities Secretariat of the League. Invariably, League officials tried in the first instance to resolve the issue in question through informal contacts with the government named

Section des commissions administratives et des questions des minorités

Figure 2.1 Administrative staff of the Minorities Commission.

in the petition. Only if this failed was the complaint referred to an ad hoc Committee of Three drawn from representatives of the League of Nations Council.[42] Subsequent discussions held with those governments subject to a petition were confidential, excluding plaintiffs' representatives. In effect, minority groups had no voice. The Committee of Three had the authority to refer cases to a full meeting of the League Council, although of the 325 petitions referred to committee level by the Minorities Secretariat, only 14 actually proceeded any further.[43] Even when this did occur, the fact that the accused state was invited to take a seat at the relevant Council session effectively ruled out any real possibility of redress, given that decisions had to be unanimous.

What is more, the complaints procedure could be highly protracted. One petition submitted in 1925 concerning Latvia's recent decision not to compensate dispossessed landowners contained

138 pages, while Latvia's response to the League was three times as long. There is no record of Latvia's answer to subsequent League advice to explore the prospect of compensation. In spite of this, the Committee of Three's review was concluded without any specific action being recommended to the League Council.[44] Such partial information and defective responses proved to be the rule rather than the exception.

At the time of the peace conference, at least some commentators had proposed that minorities in the new states should be given cultural autonomy in the form previously envisaged by Renner and Bauer. One such influential figure was the Viennese international lawyer and academic Rudolf Laun. His memorandum *Entwurf eines internationalen Vertrages über den Schutz nationaler Minderheiten* was considered at the 1919 League of Nations conference in Berne and later during the discussions leading to the St Germain peace treaty.[45] Laun's suggestions were, however, firmly rejected. In the eyes of the peacemakers, European security would be threatened by any dilution of the indivisibly sovereign nation state. Giving minorities legal personality and allowing them to create autonomous public bodies might, it was felt, lead to the formation of states within states and in extreme cases fuel irredentism.

There were indeed individuals and groups within the region who, following the logic of Max Hildebert-Boehm, were intent on undermining the 'small' states that had emerged after the war. However, for other influential commentators amongst the new national minorities, cultural autonomy was predicated precisely on respect for one's state of residence and on acceptance of its existing borders. These genuine *minority* activists could give qualified approval to the line, articulated by British foreign minister Austen Chamberlain in 1925, that 'the object of the minority treaties was to secure for the minorities that measure of protection and justice which would gradually prepare them to be *merged* in the national community to which they belonged' (emphasis added).[46] What minority leaders understood by merging, however, was simply the *integration* of different ethnic groups into an overarching state community. They emphatically rejected any suggestion that national minorities should undergo full cultural *assimilation* – a notion propounded by the League of Nations *rapporteur* on minority issues, Brazilian diplomat Afranio Mello Franco.[47]

Spearheading the attacks on Mello Franco's proposals were, among others, the Baltic Germans Paul Schiemann and Ewald Ammende. Both were by now leading lights within a European-wide minority rights movement that had begun to develop in the aftermath of the peace settlement. Ammende was born in 1890 in the port city of Pernau (Pärnu), which became part of Estonia after 1917. He was drawn to Schiemann through reading Schiemann's editorials for the liberal German newspaper *Rigasche Rundschau* during his youth. The two men met for the first time in 1918 when Ammende was salvaging what he could from his family's import–export business following the collapse of Russia. Ammende subsequently worked for a spell on the *Rigasche Rundschau*, which Schiemann resumed editing in 1919. Ammende then completed a doctorate based on extensive travels in central and Eastern Europe to study the situation of German minorities in the new states of the region.[48] This brought him into contact with other key German minority leaders, including Rudolf Brandsch, a parliamentarian from Romania. Ammende's dismay at the sense of isolation and hopelessness that he encountered while collecting thesis material amongst the scattered German populations reinforced his conviction that a new association should be formed to protect German minority interests throughout Europe.[49]

Brandsch, supported by Ammende, took the first steps in this direction by organizing a preliminary conference in Vienna attended by representatives of the 11 German minority populations from across Europe. It was, Ammende affirmed, to be 'the model for all future activities and common measures of the German minorities in Europe'.[50] The outcome of this meeting in October 1922 was a resolution committing most of those present to a common *Minoritätenpolitik*, leading to internationally agreed cultural autonomy.[51]

Preparations continued in the ensuing months for the founding congress of the *Verband der deutschen Minderheiten in Europa* (hereafter *Verband*), which eventually took place between 29 June and 2 July 1923 in Vienna. On the agenda was discussion of all aspects of the life of German minorities, including their economic situation and their problems over schooling, language and culture. The meeting instituted a standing committee comprising one representative from each of the German minority groups and made plans for the setting up of a permanent office, hopefully, in Vienna.[52]

The title chosen for the organization is instructive, and was intended to be so. By choosing the term *Minderheit* (minority) the organizers expressly acknowledged existing state borders, not least to disarm the many critics of German minority organizations. More importantly, use of the word was felt to be vital in working to influence international legislation, where the concept of minority was now rapidly establishing itself within the discourse.[53] It also pointedly distinguished the founders of the *Verband* from nationalist revisionists such as Boehm, who dismissively equated *Minderheit* (minority) with *minderwertig* (worthless).[54]

All of this was to underline that the new German organization had no intention of trying to revise the peace settlement; rather, it wished to promote a positive agenda of working to give minorities the genuine protection that they felt was not afforded to them by the existing League of Nations structures. Although the founders of the *Verband* acknowledged the importance of the League's activity in the field of minority rights, they nevertheless saw considerable room for improvement. For example, they lobbied vigorously for the establishment of a permanent standing committee that would give minority representatives the voice on the international stage that they so obviously lacked. According to Paul Schiemann, elected as *Verband* committee member for Latvia's Germans, only in this way would the League of Nations become a union of free and equal *peoples*, rather than a body for new and existing *states*, whose rights and duties were, as before, unequal.[55] Beyond this, the *Verband* committed itself from the outset to working for European-wide statutory legislation on minority rights based on the principle of cultural autonomy. That principle was seen as offering the only viable long-term guarantee against forcible assimilation of German minorities.[56]

The setting-up of the *Verband* proved to be a landmark in the history of cultural autonomy, in so far as it provided the first international platform for countering those European leaders who saw everywhere the spectre of states within states. No individual more eloquently attacked this thinking than Paul Schiemann, who was by now the leading Baltic German politician in Latvia, as well as editor of the influential liberal daily *Rigasche Rundschau*. A long-term admirer of Renner and Bauer, Schiemann was to become the most influential figure in developing and adapting their ideas to the new European realities bequeathed by the post-war peace settlement. Indeed, he soon came to be referred to by his co-workers as the 'thinker of the minorities movement'.[57]

Schiemann was no mere theorist but thoroughly involved as a member of parliament in the day-to-day political struggles in his own country, as were many if not most of his *Verband* colleagues in their respective states of residence. When it came to cultural autonomy, however, Schiemann, Ammende and other Baltic German minority activists undoubtedly benefited from the fact that a number of leading Estonian and Latvian politicians also remained favourably disposed to the idea, following their own achievements in securing independence from Russian rule. Moreover, the specific Baltic experience of Schiemann and others like him, who fully accepted their own responsibilities in helping to build up new democratic states, put him in a strong position to disarm fears that cultural autonomy would automatically undermine the unity of those countries. Nothing better exemplified Schiemann's approach than his maxim 'Politics must be for the good of the state in which one resides; any other end is suicide'.[58]

3 The Baltic arena

In the context of early 1920s Europe, the new Baltic states stood out by virtue of the unique constitutional provisions that they made for national minorities. In all three cases, legislation passed during the initial phases of independent statehood not only guaranteed the civil and ethnic rights of individual citizens but also devolved certain cultural functions – most notably administration of education – to representative bodies of organized minority groups. Estonia and Lithuania directly adopted many of the principles previously elaborated by Renner, Bauer and Dubnow. The Latvian approach was somewhat different but is nevertheless usually characterized as a form of collective cultural autonomy.[1]

It has been observed with regard to the Baltic states collectively that, 'this latitudianarism was ... unique in the world, and ... had no western models'.[2] Active lobbying by Baltic German, Jewish and other minority representatives was certainly one important factor that brought the cultural autonomy ideal to the point of realization. However, the success of these efforts was, of course, also contingent upon the support of politicians drawn from the titular national majority.

In all three countries, governments adopted at the outset of independence general provisions acknowledging the rights of minorities. Lithuania promised most, paradoxically as a result of being under German occupation from 1915, in so far as Berlin had encouraged national demands as part of a strategy for breaking up Russia and securing German dominance. The occupying German military authorities of what was designated *Land Oberost* gave recognition to no fewer than six local languages in this highly complex multi-ethnic region.[3] They also sanctioned the formation of a Lithuanian National Council (*Taryba*) in September 1917, which subsequently became the main engine of the independence movement and the key forum for discussion of the nationalities issue. Inevitably the nationalities question figured prominently on the political agenda during 1918–1920. At this time the emerging Lithuanian state faced not only the external threat of Bolshevism, but also Polish national designs on the Vilnius region.[4]

The leaders of the Lithuanian national movement claimed Vilnius as their capital on the grounds that it had once been the hub of the mediaeval and early-modern Grand Duchy of Lithuania. However, the Duchy had in no sense been a proto-national state. The Lithuanian claim underlined the impossibility in this region of resolving nationality issues territorially since the majority of those living in the Vilnius area were of Polish, Jewish, Belorussian or Russian ethnicity. Lithuanian speakers made up fewer than one in five of the population in 1918. Expediently, therefore, the Lithuanian national movement set out to win Belorussian and especially Jewish support for its programme.[5]

Backing from the Jewish population assumed a particular relevance given the international lobbying then being carried out by the *Comité des délégations juives auprès de la Conférence de la Paix*, under the leadership of the liberal Zionist Leo Motzkin. A memorandum presented to the peacemakers contributed to the pressure on the *Taryba*. The document called for full Jewish autonomy in the spheres of religion, culture and social welfare, including a separate ministry for Jewish affairs, as well as proportional representation for Jews within state institutions. Once Lithuanian foreign minister Augustinas Voldemaras accepted the main points the way was cleared for the passage in March 1920 of a law granting Jewish cultural autonomy on the basis of the traditional Jewish councils (*kehillot*).[6]

Indeed, Lithuania's Jews had already instituted 78 such local bodies by the time the new legislation officially sanctioned the process. The *kehillot* were recognized at public law and thus had the right to impose taxes and issue ordinances dealing with religious affairs, education and philanthropy. They were also responsible for registering Jewish births, marriages and deaths. The 1920 law nevertheless fell short of what Jewish leaders desired in that it failed to provide a legal basis for centralized organization at the national level. What they had instead was an informal de facto arrangement, tolerated by the government, whereby they elected a standing national council, which then worked in conjunction with the state minister for Jewish affairs.[7]

Promises of cultural autonomy for all ethnic groups were also contained in the 'manifesto to all the peoples of Estonia', adopted by the leaders of the Estonian National Council on 24 February 1918, just one day before German military occupation was extended to the entire territory of Russia's Baltic provinces. Hardly surprisingly, the occupation exacerbated long-standing tensions between Estonians and Latvians on the one hand, and the Baltic German population on the other. Under the German–Soviet treaties of Brest-Litovsk and Berlin, signed respectively in March and August 1918, the future of the Baltic territories was to be determined by the will of the people living there.[8] In practice, the voices of the Estonians and Latvians were muted as the presence of the German army encouraged conservative Baltic German elites to try to restore the dominance lost as a result of the February 1917 Revolution. 'Self-determination' thus turned out to involve consultation with a Baltic German-dominated council augmented by compliant Estonian and Latvian politicians.[9] At this point those who had proclaimed the Estonian Republic in February 1918 were either imprisoned or driven underground. It was symptomatic of this period that Paul Schiemann, already a committed liberal opponent of the landed estates (*Ritterschaften*), was forced to leave the German military zone for Berlin.[10]

Schiemann would always bitterly regret the way in which relations between his own community and the new leaders of Estonia and Latvia were further aggravated by the events following on from the end of the war and the armistice. With Germany's defeat in the First World War, national leaders were able to re-emerge in Estonia and also in neighbouring Latvia where a declaration of independence was adopted in November 1918. Like the earlier Estonian declaration, this was addressed not solely to the titular Latvian nationality but to all citizens of Latvia, who were urged 'to maintain peace and order and to support the provisional government in its difficult and responsible work'. Although the declaration referred to the 'united ethnographic boundaries' of the state, undertakings were also made to respect the ethnic rights of minority groups. A nationalities commission was established to oversee this.[11]

Under the provisions of the 11 November 1918 armistice, however, Reich German volunteer forces were allowed back into the Baltic territories as an interim defence against the advancing Soviet armies bent on retaking the area for Lenin's government at the turn of 1918–1919. Baltic Germans too were prepared to help defend the lands on which they lived; in Estonia a *Baltenregiment* was created that very soon operated under the umbrella of the rapidly improvised Estonian national army. In the more volatile political conditions of Latvia, the Baltic German *Landeswehr* pursued its own agenda, notwithstanding its undoubted role in keeping the Bolsheviks at bay. Not until the defeat of German forces in June 1919 at the hands of a joint Estonian–Latvian force were Baltic German liberals able to come back into play in Latvia. Their path was eased by the fact that the remaining political power of the old German elites was broken by the draconian agrarian reforms of the new Baltic governments during 1919–1920.

As the agrarian laws showed only too well, many within the Baltic national movements saw the attainment of statehood as a means of prioritizing the rights of the ethnic majority following centuries of oppression at the hands of foreign overlords. Even after military victory had been attained there remained a deep-seated sense of insecurity and resentment amongst more nation-ally minded Estonian, Latvian and Lithuanian political elites, occasioned by the perceived threat of neighbouring great powers and the continued influential position occupied by minorities within the new states.

Nationalizing impulses proved hardest to resist in Lithuania. Poland's annexation of Vilnius in October 1920 and, later, the dispute with Germany over Memel (Klaipeda) gave the politics of the early independence period 'a far more explicitly and shrilly nationalistic tinge than was the case in Estonia and Latvia'.[12] As the prospect of reclaiming Vilnius receded during the early 1920s, so the Lithuanian state attached correspondingly less importance to the rights of Jews living within its existing borders. Indeed, the liberal provisions for Jewish autonomy put in place during 1919–1920 were already being undermined by the time Lithuania drafted its first formal constitution in 1922.

The promise in this document to allow the establishment of centralized institutions of cultural autonomy was never fully real-ized. Conservative nationalist politicians such as Voldemaras, who had championed Jewish cultural autonomy at the start of independence, found themselves marginalized politically after the elections of 1922 when power passed to a Christian democratic bloc that was rather less well disposed to the concept of public corporate organization for minority groups. Opponents of autonomy had little difficulty in exploiting internal divisions within the Jewish community and thereby contriving to bring about the abolition of the existing *kehillot* by the start of 1926, even before the eclipse of liberal democracy in Lithuania in December of that same year. The new head of state installed after the 1926 nationalist coup, Antanas Smetona, had been one of those conservative politicians who had originally favoured cultural autonomy for Lithuania's Jews. While residual traces of this sentiment can be found in Smetona's continuing support for Jewish schooling, autonomy as envisaged at the start of the decade was now effectively a lost cause.

This is not something that could be said of neighbouring Latvia, despite inevitable pressure from more nationalistically minded forces at the start of the 1920s. For these, Latvia's recognition by the Western powers and the League of Nations in 1921 was seen as opening up the possibility for a more assertive line towards national minority groups.[13] Some confirmation of this came from a memorandum addressed by the Paris-based *Comité des délégations juives* to the League in April 1922, claiming that the Latvian government had failed to deliver on the promise of equal treatment before the law for all residents, regardless of ethnicity:

> The Latvian government protests against the claims [of our memorandum] that the Jews are subject to persecution in Latvia which to some extent recalls the persecution perpetrated by the former [T]sarist regime, and insists that these assertions are baseless.... We will restrict ourselves to citing the fact that ... tens of thousands of Jews who have lived in this country for years, even decades, and in some cases were even born in Latvia but who because of the war were forcibly displaced from their homeland and exiled in the far off provinces of Russia, are now prevented by the Latvian government from returning home.[14]

Nevertheless, the balance of political forces within Latvia's new institutions precluded the complete abandonment of the liberal ideals enshrined in the original declarations of independence.[15] By December 1919, Latvia had placed on the statute book a framework law for the schooling of minorities allowing minority representatives to manage their own schooling in their own language. The original intention was to enshrine these provisions in Latvia's new constitution, which came into force on 7 November 1922. This made reference to a single political 'nation of Latvia' (*Latvijas tauta*), while stating that ethnic Latvians (*Latviešu tauta*) were only one of a number of sovereign and autonomous ethnic communities entitled to preserve their distinct cultural heritage, religion and language.[16] However, the second part of the constitution, elaborating in detail civic and other rights, failed to secure a majority in the Latvian parliament. As a result there was no formal constitutional basis for the exercise of minority cultural autonomy.

National minorities thus had to content themselves for the moment with the 1919 schooling law. Even so, because this was a framework law it gave considerable scope for autonomous cultural development. According to its terms minority schools were essentially under the supervision of their own separate administration, physically located within Latvia's ministry of education. The heads of these administrations, although in effect civil servants, were actually chosen by the parliamentary delegates of the minority in question and simply put forward for approval by the government.[17] For a number of reasons, not least the demands of building up a Latvian language educational system virtually from scratch, subsequent governments during the 1920s generally allowed leeway to minority representatives, particularly in matters of curriculum development and inspection.[18]

An even greater degree of latitude was afforded to national minorities in Estonia where the early government honoured the founding commitment to respect the cultural rights of all peoples living within the new state. Accordingly, regulations on elementary schooling embraced the principle of instruction in the mother tongue, as did the corresponding law on secondary schooling adopted in December 1922. In districts where there were 20 or more pupils belonging to a particular linguistic minority the state was obliged to provide schooling in the relevant language.[19] Despite the bitterness caused by the actions of the Baltic German *Landeswehr* during 1919, the Estonian constituent assembly convened in that year narrowly reaffirmed the right of *all* national minorities to establish institutions for cultural self-government.[20]

The promises enshrined in the 1920 Constitution were finally honoured in February 1925 with the passage of the law on cultural autonomy for national minorities. This allowed representatives of Estonia's largest minorities (Germans, Russians, Swedes) and of any other group numbering more than 3,000 to establish their own corporations at public law and, on this basis, to set up self-governments with responsibility for schooling and other cultural matters.

The view that Lithuania's corresponding provisions for the Jewish minority brought to 'the modern national state ... the archaic principle of corporate autonomy for social and religious groups, characteristic in western medieval Christendom' has been echoed in the case of Estonia's 1925 law.[21] Certainly, conservative notions of *ständische Gesellschaft* dear to the Baltic Germans were perpetuated after 1918.[22] However, while long-standing traditions clearly did guide the thinking of some of the leading proponents of Estonia's cultural autonomy, the provisions of the 1925 law appear more consistent with the more progressive, liberal individualist vision previously articulated by Renner and Bauer.

This is apparent above all in the emphasis on one's national identity being a matter of free choice. The choice operated at two levels. First, the 1920 Constitution stipulated the right of each individual citizen to choose and, if so desired, to change the ethnicity recorded in his or her passport. However, under the provisions of the law of 1925, declaring a particular ethnicity did not in itself entail commitment to membership of the public corporation established in the name of the relevant group. Rather, such a corporation could only be established on the basis of 50 per cent of the citizens belonging to the relevant minority consenting to have their names included on an electoral register. Once this was drawn up, elections could take place to a cultural council. This would constitute the legislative arm of minority self-government. Even then, a cultural council could only be established if half of the registered voters participated in the elections. Only at that point would the newly elected council be in a position to implement cultural autonomy, providing that at least two-thirds of its members voted in favour.

It is the pronounced emphasis on personal choice that distinguishes Estonia's legislation from the corresponding Lithuanian law on Jewish autonomy. In the latter case there was no formal requirement to enrol on a national register; everyone of Jewish nationality within a relevant district could take part in elections to the local Jewish *kehilla*. Moreover, once this had been constituted all local Jews automatically became liable to pay taxes for cultural purposes, regardless of whether or not they had actually voted for setting up a *kehilla*.[23] The only possible escape from this obligation was formally to renounce Jewish nationality. In Estonia, by contrast, only those voluntarily enrolled on the national register were liable to pay taxes to the cultural self-government after it had been established. Avoiding this obligation required no more than a written declaration of intent to leave the national register, albeit on the understanding that all benefits of membership were relinquished in so doing. The constituency of minority cultural self-government in Estonia thus derived very much from acts of 'deliberate personal will of individual nationals living within the state territory'.[24]

As in Latvia, the initial impetus behind Estonia's cultural autonomy came primarily from the ranks of the minorities themselves. Indeed, ethnic German representatives brought detailed proposals to the 1919–1920 constituent assembly, where they worked alongside Swedish and Russian representatives to secure the constitutional stipulation that 'members of national minorities living in Estonia may establish their own autonomous institutions in the interests of their national culture and welfare, in so far as this does not go against the interests of the state'.[25]

Estonia's numerically small Jewish community was unable to secure representation in the constituent assembly. A congress of Jewish communities held in Tallinn in May 1919 nevertheless endorsed the principle of non-territorial cultural autonomy. At this meeting, delegate Sergei Eisenstadt, in particular, conveyed eloquently the ideas of Renner and Bauer, stressing as key principles the belonging of an autonomous minority to the state in which it resides and the 'inviolable' unity of the citizen body.[26] Jewish representatives subsequently liaised with the *Deutsch-Baltische Partei in Estland* (hereinafter DBP), the sole parliamentary voice of Baltic Germans in Estonia, as it prepared to present an initial bill on cultural autonomy to Estonia's first *Riigikogu* (parliament) in the spring of 1921.[27]

The architects of Estonia's 1925 law were, however, far from confined to the ranks of the minorities. Leading Estonian public figures also threw their weight behind the initial proposals. By far the most prominent of these was Konstantin Päts, leader of Estonia's Agrarian Party and previously head of the Estonian provisional government of November 1918 to May 1919. Some authors even see Päts as the true father of the Estonian cultural autonomy law.[28] Already within the constituent assembly Päts had defended the Baltic German proposals against the now familiar cry that they would create a 'state within a state'.[29] He also endorsed the initial bill presented to the *Riigikogu* in April 1921.

As the main representative of the Estonian conservative right, Päts was the least ill disposed to the German former ruling class. In this respect he was also inclined to see political nationhood not as an amalgam of individual citizens, but as deriving from a state of equilibrium between different social groups. This was a view that had been impressed upon him by the example of Finland's estates-based Diet during the period 1863–1906.[30] It also seems likely, however, that Päts became conversant with the ideas of Renner and Bauer through conversations with Baltic German liberal Heinrich Pantenius during the early 1900s when Päts was inclined politically towards the radical left.[31]

Admittedly, Päts' thinking on autonomy was also partly dictated by considerations of realpolitik. Having characterized Estonia's agrarian laws of 1919 as geopolitically naïve, he would later assert that ethnic Germans and Russians living in Estonia were not simply members of a minority but extended representatives of neighbouring 'great nations' who had to be accommodated within the Estonian state.[32] In a similar vein, many Estonian politicians no doubt saw cultural autonomy as a means of deflecting international propaganda by dispossessed German landowners who sought to blacken Estonia's reputation at the League of Nations and amongst European opinion more broadly.[33]

Cultivating a positive international image remained a crucial factor even after Estonia's entry to the League of Nations. However, there was nothing in the League stipulations on minority rights that obliged Estonia to adopt such far-reaching provisions for cultural autonomy. Such arrangements actually ran counter to the prevailing thinking on minority rights within League circles, where cultural autonomy was still seen in terms of creating states within states.[34] Thus, realpolitik alone does not offer a sufficient explanation for the developments of the early 1920s.

It is difficult then to deny that genuine conviction lay at the heart of the commitment to cultural autonomy during the formative years of the Estonian Republic. The source of that conviction can be found in the ideas of one of the nineteenth-century founding fathers of the Estonian national movement, Jakob Hurt. His maxim, that since Estonians could never be great in number they should aspire to greatness through their culture, finds striking echoes in the later *Riigikogu* debates on whether or not to pass a law on cultural autonomy. Even those Estonian social democrats most hostile to the Baltic German former privileged elite could still recognize that the passage of the law would put Estonia ahead 'of the biggest democratic states and the entire world'.[35]

The attempt to overcome past grievances and look towards the future is a striking feature of the *Riigikogu* debates over cultural autonomy. Responding to repeated reminders of 700 years of servitude under the Baltic Germans, parliamentary rapporteur Ado Anderkopp observed that 'we do not produce laws with an eye to proving how much we have suffered in the past, but in order to give to others the freedoms we wish to enjoy ourselves'.[36] In saying this, Anderkopp was responding to claims by social democrat Karl Ast that the former German overlords had not yet reconciled themselves to the existence of an independent Estonia. Yet even Ast was alive to the historic significance of what was being proposed:

> The Social Democrats are pleased that this law has been put forward since it derives from the work of Springer (Renner) and Bauer. We would be happy to see Estonia become a modern democracy which in its approach to the national question applies a set of principles wholly different to those employed by the old democracies. We already know that the latter offer no cause for celebration as far as the development of the national question is concerned. Despite everything that was said before and during the Versailles treaty, European democracy has done nothing as far as peoples' rights to self-determination are concerned; rather, old methods still prevail to the same extent.[37]

While cultural autonomy by its nature found advocates on both the left and the right of the political spectrum, there was no unanimity within any of Estonia's main political parties. That much can be seen from the fact that it took fully four years from the initial Baltic German proposal to the final passage of the law.

Opposition was most pronounced within the ranks of the Estonian People's Party, headed by Jaan Tõnisson, which had become the successor to the radical anti-German wing of the late-nineteenth-century national movement. Telling in this regard is Tõnisson's allegation that:

> Ruling circles [amongst the Germans] seem bent on setting up German colonies as most of the German elements in the Baltic lands have always been. They have always been keen to prevent encroachment from outside; in a way this has been our good fortune, since it has prevented our assimilation.[38]

For Tõnisson these archaic forms now had to give way to a new and unitary nation state. Equally, many social democrats, while sympathetic to cultural autonomy as we saw above, were just as suspicious of the motives of the Baltic German community.

Indeed, many if not most Baltic Germans found it difficult to come to terms with their ascribed status as but one of several minorities within an Estonian dominated state. During the autonomy debates German representatives repeatedly insisted that their community's importance could not be measured numerically, but rather had to reflect its historic role in the Baltic provinces. In the words of former estate owner Baron von Stackelberg: 'We never should nor will be measurable according to our number.'[39] No lovers of the new democratic parliamentary republic, Stackelberg and others remained at heart wedded to the hierarchical, corporate structures that had served their caste so well over centuries. Stackelberg was thus far from untypical in viewing autonomy as a means of recreating a corporate organic community amongst the Baltic Germans, while at the same time bitterly regretting having to adopt 'sterile democratic, mechanistic' methods of administration to achieve this goal.[40]

The initial proposals put forward by Baltic German leaders in January 1921 tried in vain to circumvent parliamentary procedures entirely, arguing that the cultural autonomy promised in Article 21 of Estonia's Constitution could and should be implemented simply on the basis of governmental decree.[41] The German draft bill presented three months later to the *Riigikogu* was drawn up by a committee chaired by Eduard von Bodisco, a man who also headed the association of expropriated German landowners. This initial draft accepted the principle of free choice of nationality but envisaged that cultural autonomy would not be established on the basis of voluntary enrolment to a register; rather, it would automatically encompass all Germans living in Estonia. The draft also expressed a strong preference for the competencies of minority self-government being extended beyond culture to encompass, among other things, social welfare.[42]

Such thinking was hardly calculated to appease Estonian opponents of cultural autonomy. The Baltic German proposal quickly became bogged down in a series of parliamentary committees and was condemned as inimical to the democratic spirit of the new Estonia. It was to rebut this charge that the DBP chairman August Spindler composed a long memorandum for members of the *Riigikogu*. Depicting cultural autonomy as a logical outcome of liberal democratic thinking, Spindler now conceded that the competencies of the proposed self-governments should be confined strictly to matters of culture. Furthermore, he rebutted suggestions that autonomy would lead to states within states by reminding the *Riigikogu* that powers were to be delegated to cultural self-governments by the state itself. The state would also retain broad supervisory powers, as well as providing the bulk of the funding for autonomous minority institutions.[43]

Spindler's overall argument was that there need be no inherent conflict of interest between the proposed autonomous national bodies and the central state authorities. Those who did not grasp this reality, he suggested, simply failed to understand the proper functions of the state.[44] Echoing Renner and Bauer, Spindler stressed that majoritarian democracy was appropriate when it concerned matters of common interest to the entire population of a state. Yet the same spirit of democracy precluded coercing individuals or groups in those spheres concerning them alone. Culture, like religion, was an obvious example of this. Acknowledging this reality through the medium of cultural autonomy, far from engendering irredentism, would reduce the risk of national groups aspiring to form states within states.[45] Punctuating his analysis with references to Renner and Bauer and other key figures from the liberal–socialist camp, Spindler recalled the words of the German Independent Socialist Lebedour to the *Reichstag* in October 1918: 'The principle of cultural autonomy must once and for all apply in all countries.'[46]

How representative Spindler's views were among Estonia's Germans is obviously open to debate, given the views of people like Stackelberg. Nevertheless, Ewald Ammende's activities within the *Verband der deutschen Minderheiten in Europa* had already proved the existence of liberal elements more willing to accept the new realities of the post-war Europe, harsh as they seemed. One such example was the Tartu-based headmaster and political activist Heinrich Pantenius. Having already become familiar with the ideas of Renner and Bauer during the early 1900s, Pantenius declared in December 1920 that 'naturally the Baltic Germans have to renounce all forms of privilege and domination'.[47] In such quarters it was better understood that the only way to ensure the long-term survival of one's culture was to accept national minority status, embrace and utilize democratic parliamentary procedures and work in this way for the overall good of the state to which one had been consigned by history.

Ultimately, the case put forward in Spindler's memorandum failed to convince his Estonian opponents of the virtues of cultural autonomy. In the very month he published his arguments, March 1922, a sub-commission of the *Riigikogu* concluded that it was still not practicable to draft a definitive law regulating the question of autonomy. Significantly, it was Konstantin Päts, by now again prime minister, who intervened to break the impasse by proposing in the first instance a loose framework law.[48] With interior minister Ado Anderkopp he then co-authored a second draft law, which was duly presented to an open session of parliament in March 1923. Unlike the original Baltic German project, the Päts/Anderkopp proposals provided for voluntary enrolment on a national register and tried as far as possible formally to delimit the competencies of the institutions and their relationship to the state.[49]

One obvious objection to the new bill was that its clauses were still too vague. In response its authors reminded their parliamentary colleagues of the sheer novelty of the enterprise, which made this inevitably a step into the unknown. Other arguments against the bill's passage barely concealed more fundamental concerns. In particular, the government's desire to get the legislation through was seen as yielding to external pressures generated by the Berlin-based lawyer Baron von Heyking and other former Baltic German landowners who were bent on internationalizing the question of land reform and making the case for this being an infringement of minority rights rather than a question of social justice.[50]

On the other hand, there were opponents of the bill who accepted the need for minority schooling but disputed placing this under the control of a cultural self-government. They justified their position by pointing to the already existing network of minority-language schools operating in Estonia on the basis of the general education law. The fact that Estonian-language schools often had many more pupils per class than their German-language counterparts understandably also fuelled popular resentment. Jaan Tõnisson, in particular, seized on this point to warn that granting cultural autonomy would consolidate the gulf between German- and Estonian-language schools, bringing with it the risk that ethnic Estonian parents would favour the former over the latter.[51]

Tõnisson's claim has some foundation, in that funding for schools was contingent upon the number of classes rather than upon student numbers. At the same time, this objection signally failed to take account of the geographically dispersed nature of Baltic German settlements, which made it impossible in many districts to find the required number of pupils to justify establishing a class. Protests of this sort, railing at extra rights for minorities, also overlooked the crucially important point that under cultural autonomy such rights carried additional duties. Not the least of these was the requirement to pay extra taxation for the cultural and schooling needs of the relevant national community.

The debates on the revised autonomy bill of 1923, presented in the dying days of the first *Riigikogu*, were both intense and prolonged. Although the law was eventually passed at first reading, the parliamentary deputies voted against putting it forward for the second and third readings necessary to get it onto the statute book. Instead the bill was referred back to the committee level for further elaboration. The delays that this strategy occasioned generated great bitterness among minority representatives, who stressed, above all, the urgent need to start rebuilding their schooling networks.[52] Despite this there were further disappointments during the remaining months of 1923. After the second *Riigikogu* convened, Tõnisson's People's Party resumed its efforts to obstruct the passage of the law. Its tactic in this instance was to propose that instead of allowing one centralized body of cultural self-government for each eligible minority, cultural autonomy should be organized locally under the supervision of existing municipal governments. From a minority point of view, however, this threatened to defeat the entire purpose of the exercise.[53]

These and other differences were only resolved after a key meeting in March 1924 between Tõnisson and the Baltic German representatives Ewald Ammende and Werner Hasselblatt. The outcome was broad agreement that the competencies of the autonomous organizations had to be strictly confined to the cultural sphere, thus excluding not only social welfare, but also church affairs, which many Baltic Germans had felt should be included within the framework of cultural autonomy. In return, Tõnisson consented to the establishment of centralized cultural self-governments, albeit democratically elected on the basis of local constituencies. A number of practical issues, including that of the national register, remained to be resolved, but even the Baltic German press now acknowledged that Tõnisson and his party were ready to resolve the autonomy issue quickly. The March 1924 meeting, which rounded off with an agreed written communication, can thus be regarded as the critical turning point in the passage of legislation on cultural autonomy.[54] Not even the fall of Konstantin Päts' latest government, which had again thrown its weight behind the new legislation, could disrupt the more measured tone of the debate that became apparent after March 1924. Ambiguities were removed from the text of a new bill and it passed its first reading on 7 June 1924 with an overwhelming majority[55]

In rebuking the new government for devoting only one sentence of its programme to the question of cultural autonomy, Agrarian Party parliamentarian and former interior minister Karl Einbund had reminded incoming Prime Minister Friedrich Akel that the nationality question would only be solved by fostering a common civic identity on the part of all Estonia's residents.[56] When in June 1924 the social democrat Juhan Jans characterized Baltic Germans as *déclassé* nobles rather than a national minority, and equated them with communists as a threat to the Estonian state, Werner Hasselblatt rebuked Jans for his 'spiteful and suspicious' comments. Hasselblatt emphasized that nourishing the diverse ethnic cultures within Estonia's population was essential to the welfare of the new state and of its citizens. Recalling his own experiences in late Tsarist Russia, Hasselblatt asked how many of those assembled, be they German or Estonian, had like him been denied the 'privilege' of education in their mother tongue.[57]

More immediately, Hasselblatt reminded his opponent of Baltic Germans' service in fighting the Soviet invasion of 1918, thereby

Figure 3.1 Werner Hasselblatt.

eliciting cheers from the parliamentary floor. One thing that undoubtedly bound most Estonian and Baltic German politicians was a profound aversion to Bolshevism. Their commonalty on this subject was soon confirmed beyond all doubt by the solidarity shown to the state by Germans on 1 December 1924 when several hundred well-armed communist insurgents mounted a failed putsch in Tallinn. There could hardly have been a more timely reminder of the importance of bringing all citizens of Estonia together. The episode therefore provided the final impetus for the adoption of the law on cultural autonomy, which quickly passed its second and third readings in February 1925.[58]

The abortive communist putsch in Tallinn was not without effect on the parallel struggle for cultural autonomy then taking place in Latvia. In agreeing to support emergency legislation tabled by the new government of Hugo Celmiņš, Paul Schiemann and the German fraction which he headed secured in return a promise to support the cultural autonomy projects that had been elaborated by Latvia's various minority groups during the preceding four years. While Baltic Germans in particular had profited from the 1919 law on minority schooling, their leaders had retained a desire for a full law on cultural autonomy, albeit for different motives. In this respect the liberal/conservative divide already noted in Estonia was far more apparent among the Baltic Germans of Latvia, where most viewed cultural autonomy not primarily in terms of minority rights but rather as a vehicle for preserving their own exclusivity and indeed perceived superiority vis-à-vis other national groups.[59]

At the other end of the political spectrum, Paul Schiemann argued for cultural autonomy on liberal grounds, treating Baltic Germans as but one of the national groups who had to work for the good of the new Latvia.[60] In contrast to the situation in Estonia, divisions within Latvian Germandom had to be accommodated in no fewer than six political parties. That it was possible to set differences aside, at least in the parliamentary arena, owed much to Schiemann's charismatic leadership, though many on the right in particular saw him as an unavoidable evil in the new and to them unwelcome parliamentary era.[61] The attitude of the old Baltic German elites was best exemplified by their insistence on separate autonomy laws for each minority group living in Latvia. Between 1921 and 1925 this remained the formal position of the German fraction, although it did communicate regularly with other minority representatives and each group promised mutual support for their respective projects. Cooperation was particularly close between Baltic German and Jewish political representatives.[62] However, the Jewish minority was itself by no means immune to the kind of internal political differences that were so readily apparent within the German camp.

Latvia's Jewish community had begun to discuss the question of cultural autonomy as early as 1919. Represented as it also was by six different political parties within the constituent assembly, the Jewish political elite was riddled with factional disagreements. Broadly speaking, these pitted the Zionist camp – itself subdivided along religious–secular and left–right lines – and the socialist *Bund* (a subdivision of the Latvian Social Democratic Party) against the religiously orthodox *Agudat Israel*. The different groups all supported the principle of Jewish autonomy, and further agreed that this should be administered by means of a public corporation. How to define the boundaries of the Jewish national community, however, was the subject of intense debate. All agreed that autonomous institutions could not embrace anyone of another religious faith, and yet, as in Lithuania, there was disagreement over whether a Jewish national register should automatically encompass everyone born into the Jewish faith, or rather be constituted on the basis of voluntary adhesion. The question was, of course, linked to the issue of whether the corporation should levy compulsory taxation on its members, or alternatively whether to rely on voluntary donations to supplement state and municipal funding.[63]

Mirroring the Baltic German predicament, there were also disagreements between Jewish groups over the scope of autonomy. Following the line of Renner and Bauer, the socialist *Bund* advocated a purely cultural autonomy, arguing that other aspects of the national question would be solved through the creation of a socialist order. Other parties argued that autonomous institutions should have a more extensive range of competences. Obviously of great relevance to the Jewish minority was the issue of religion. Whereas the *Bund* and a section of the Zionist camp argued for a purely secular autonomy, *Agudat Israel* threatened to withdraw support and establish its own register unless autonomy also incorporated Jewish religious institutions.[64]

Especially contentious, however, was the question of which language or languages should serve as the medium of instruction in Jewish schools. Whereas Zionist parties argued for education in Hebrew – or at least for parity between Hebrew and the Yiddish vernacular – the *Bund* adopted a resolutely pro-Yiddish stance. By contrast, the National Democrats, representing the more assimilated Jewish middle class, argued that German and Russian – hitherto the main languages of Jewish education in the territories of the new Latvia – should continue to be media of instruction in Jewish schools.[65]

Such differences within and between the various nationality groups also impeded the efforts of Schiemann and others to forge a united front of minority parliamentarians in favour of cultural autonomy. Advocates of autonomy were thus greatly disadvantaged once various legislative drafts began to go through the parliamentary and committee process from 1921 onwards. Indeed, by 1923 Schiemann had all but accepted that there was no immediate prospect of securing parliamentary support for cultural autonomy. Disappointment within the German community was alleviated at least partly by the creation in that same year of a new organization devoted exclusively to social, cultural and other non-political activities, the *Deutsch–Baltische Zentrale*. Although a private corporation rather than the public body advocated by Renner and Bauer, the new organization promised to give much needed experience in managing national minority affairs.[66]

Schiemann and the German fraction nevertheless continued the struggle to gain parliamentary approval for a separate German autonomy project of the kind adopted in Estonia in February 1925, the passage of which gave the liberal camp additional leverage in their dealings with Baltic German conservatives in Latvia. This much is clear from the emotionally charged meeting between the German faction leaders on 20 November 1925, a mere few days after the Estonian Germans held the inaugural meeting of their newly established cultural council (see Chapter 4). Among the reasons Schiemann advanced for concentrating on a similar general law for all of Latvia's minorities was the resistance of the Latvian Social Democrat Party to any separate German law. The social democratic stance was also supported by Jewish groups, anxious that otherwise the German community might secure preferential treatment.[67] In any case, Schiemann's advocacy for a general law was met by a heated outburst from the leader of the German conservative faction Baron Wilhelm Fircks, who voiced his distaste for receiving autonomy as the 'gift of those [left] Latvian groups with which we are unable to work in the long run'. Fircks also referred to the 'odium' of inclusion with the Russians and Jews.[68] Karl Keller, who headed the German schooling section within Latvia's ministry of education, voiced his own distaste at the prospect of being 'tossed in the same barrel with the others'.[69] Schiemann for his part doggedly insisted that the recent death of the well-disposed Latvian minister Zigfrīds Meierovics, together with the fact that no law would make it through parliament without the support of the social democrats, rendered the prospect of any separate German project impossible for the foreseeable future.[70]

Schiemann's strategy had the virtue of keeping open the option of a general law on cultural autonomy, which in turn helped to head off more serious divisions within the Latvian German community. Although parliamentary opposition continued to prevent the passage of any such legislation, the position of Latvia's minorities remained far more favourable than in any of the other successor states of the region except Estonia. The situation owed much to the far-reaching implications of the 1919 law on minority schooling with its provisions for German and other minority

Figure 3.2 Paul Schiemann.

representatives to be consulted on all cultural matters particular to their community. Equally, the frustration of Latvia's Germans at not being allowed to form a public law corporation did not prevent them from replicating on a private basis through the *Zentrale* many of the features of the experiment in cultural self-government upon which Estonia's Germans embarked in the autumn of 1925.[71]

4 The practice of autonomy

Baron von Stackelberg's distaste at having to follow what he termed the 'sterile democratic mechanistic' route to corporate organization under Estonia's 1925 autonomy law tacitly recognized the divisions that existed within his own small and formerly exclusive Baltic German community. Even those Germans in favour of cultural autonomy can have had no illusions about the scale of the task involved in setting up a cultural self-government. Whatever reservations there were did not prevent the leaders of the Estonian Germans from moving promptly to implement the provisions of the law following its final ratification by parliament on 12 February 1925. Just three days later, a delegate meeting of the Deutsch-Baltische Partei (DBP) resolved to seek official approval for the establishment of German cultural self-government. To this end, various party members, including August Spindler, Heinrich Pantenius and Harry Koch, formed a preparatory commission to consider the many practical issues that were bound to arise.[1] Realizing that many if not most Estonian Germans were unclear about the process, commission members offered to make themselves available to give talks and lectures to the wider public.[2]

Once German leaders had presented their application and gained governmental approval, the first major challenge they faced was to draw up an accurate register of those entitled to vote in elections for a German cultural council. Ironically, this task fell to Werner Hasselblatt, whose preference was for compulsory rather than voluntary affiliation to a German national register.[3] Hasselblatt joined interior ministry representative Eugen Madisson and Estonian court official H. Siimer in an electoral commission set up for the purpose.[4]

The law on cultural autonomy stipulated that a list of those citizens already registered as having German nationality (taken from records held by the police) be made available for public scrutiny for a period of two months. During this time anyone not wishing to be included on a national register could apply to have his or her name struck from the list. Conversely, it was open to individual citizens to opt for German nationality and to request inclusion.[5]

The start of the statutory period of public scrutiny quickly gave rise to a discussion around who could legitimately claim belonging to a German national group in the Estonia of the 1920s. The terms of the 1925 law were not always immediately clear even to those charged with drawing up the national register. This, it has to be said, was a highly complex undertaking involving the collection of data by numerous sub-committees working at the local level. Thus, an official of the electoral commission had to explain to one local committee that 'we do not wish to register ... [Jews]..., since we are only recording Germans [i.e. persons who had indicated German nationality], irrespective of whether a person's children attend German schools'.[6]

Other observers feared that not everyone recorded on the initial list of those with German nationality actually considered themselves German. One newspaper report from July 1925 claimed that as many as 2,000 people on the list of German voters were actually Estonian, Russian or Finnish but held German nationality because their identity documents dated from the period of occupation by the Reich during 1918.[7] By the same token, in the fraught atmosphere of the immediate post-independence years, not all citizens of Estonia who were culturally German necessarily wished to advertise the fact.[8]

From the point of view of realizing cultural autonomy it was imperative to maximize the number of individuals on the list who were actively committed to this goal and who could, therefore, be relied upon to vote in elections to a cultural council; achieving the participation rate of over 50 per cent demanded by the law was paramount. All those who did not consider themselves culturally German – passport nationality notwithstanding – were, therefore, urged to strike their names from the list during the two-month period of scrutiny. Equally, those who favoured autonomy but were not officially German by nationality were encouraged to amend their personal identity documents so as to allow for their inclusion on the electoral list. Ultimately, as one internal memorandum noted, it did not matter whether people on the list were 'Estonian' or 'half-Russian': what mattered was a willingness to participate and to assume a 'responsibility for our future'.[9]

Maximizing the number of those actively committed to German culture was all the more important given that the names on the electoral list would form the basis of the national register. This would in turn be used to determine who paid taxes to the German cultural self-government. Not surprisingly, encouraging people to adopt German nationality was a contentious issue for many Estonian state officials. For instance, Johannes Beermann, head of the German schools section within Estonia's education ministry, first advised applicants for German nationality to go through his office, to bypass difficulties in registering with the local police. Soon afterwards, however, he felt obliged to withdraw this advice on the grounds that a large number of applicants might attract adverse comment.[10]

As it transpired, registering the requisite number of persons did not prove to be difficult. Already by 7 June 1925, Werner Hasselblatt could record with satisfaction that the 'overwhelming majority of our people unanimously embrace the idea of cultural autonomy'.[11] The 1922 census had recorded 18,319 people as having German nationality. Of these, 11,989 were of voting age. To meet the 50 per cent enrolment requirement of the 1925 law, the electoral commission was, therefore, obliged to enlist just less than 6,000 individuals to the electoral register. Between May and September 1925 it was actually able to collect 11,562 names, equivalent to 97 per cent of eligible ethnic Germans registered under the census.[12] One list compiled by the Estonian ministry of the interior contains details of 170 persons who adopted German nationality within the specified time. Of these, the majority (122) had previously indicated Estonian nationality, with the remainder being Latvian (19), Swedish (12), 'Baltic' (four), Russian (two), Danish (four), Polish (two), Lithuanian (one), French (two), Swiss (one) and 'unknown'.[13] In early August 1925, the Estonian newspaper *Vaba Maa* claimed that over 600 people in Tallinn alone had applied to have their names added to the German electoral list, and pointedly remarked on the high number of Estonian surnames to be found thereon.[14]

With the register in place, elections to a German cultural council (*Kulturrat*) were held on 3–5 October 1925. There were ten electoral constituencies based on existing county (*Maakond*) boundaries, subdivided into a total of 67 smaller electoral districts. The overall number of mandates per constituency was dependent upon the size of the local German population. This provision meant that Tallinn and its surrounding county of Harjumaa provided more than one-third (16) of the 41 deputies to the cultural council, whereas Tartu elected eight, Virumaa and Pärnu three, Järvamaa, Läänemaa, Viljandimaa, Saaremaa, Võrumaa and Petserimaa two each and Valgamaa one.[15]

The electoral system adopted in 1925 was bewildering in its complexity. Candidates were arranged into lists of three, some of which represented identifiable groupings, each with their own electoral platform, others of which consisted of independent candidates. Individual candidates could appear on more than one list. Voters in larger constituencies had several lists to choose from – too many according to some critics – while in some smaller constituencies there was only one list available. Having opted for a particular list, voters then had to rank the three candidates, their first choice receiving one vote, the second half a vote and the third one-third of a vote. Votes for individual candidates were then added up and seats on the council allocated according to the final ranking. In sum, as one local journalist later observed, the system was neither a normal list system nor a procedure for choosing an individual, but a mixture of both, combining the deficiencies of both.[16] Despite this, 67 per cent of eligible voters turned out at the start of October 1925 to elect from 64 separate candidate lists the first German cultural council.[17]

The council convened on 1 November 1925 in the House of the Blackheads on Pikk Street in Tallinn, one of the traditional symbols of past Baltic German dominion. Between 12.00 and 1.30, 38 council members together with invited guests took their seats in the so-called White Room. Present at the opening ceremony were Prime Minister Konstantin Päts as well as Interior Minister Karl Einbund, Foreign Minister Ado Birk and Education Minister August Rei. They were joined by the German ambassador and various journalists.[18] All present acknowledged the profound historic significance of the event. Einbund for his part underlined the importance of this 'big idea' for 'the internal development of our state'. As to the wider international resonance of implementing cultural autonomy 'for the first time in the history of the world', Foreign minister Birk went so far as to describe the example set by the German minority as vital to maintaining peace in Europe.[19] More prosaically, August Rei reminded the audience of the real reason for setting up the cultural council. 'I see among the members of the cultural council', he said, 'a large number of worthy schoolmen whom the education ministry has learned to value.'[20] Teachers were indeed prominent, alongside lawyers and other professionals.

Once the state officials had left the room, the assembled German council had to vote formally on whether to implement cultural autonomy. It quickly became clear that for all concerned this was still a huge step into the unknown. Stackelberg, speaking for the more conservative element, reiterated his concern that the new arrangements would be no more than a pale imitation of the old corporate structures which had provided the basis for Baltic German hegemony during the Tsarist era. He, therefore, argued that in opting for cultural autonomy the German community should emphasize that throughout history Germans had been the sole 'mediator, bearer and representative' of Western European culture in the Baltic area.[21] Most telling perhaps was Baron Greinert's claim that if the council really went ahead with cultural autonomy, future generations would feel themselves not as Baltic Germans but merely as part of a minority![22]

For all this, pragmatism, not to say hard realism, won the day. The majority, albeit with obvious reluctance on the part of some, acknowledged having to adapt to radically changed sociopolitical circumstances. At this stage of the proceedings the main concern of those present focused on the ambiguous nature of the framework law. It left unresolved, among other things, the crucial question of the nature and extent of state funding for German schools. Without further state legislation in such key areas, it was felt that the autonomy project might even now prove unworkable.[23]

The decisive voice proved to be that of Werner Hasselblatt. He reminded the assembled council that the law was wholly unprecedented; it was the first attempt to put into practice an ideal 'for which all Germans had struggled'. The Estonian state, he maintained, recognized the need to advance the work of the cultural council, and thus its members had no reason to doubt that continued collaboration with the authorities would give rise to positive results. Hasselblatt also urged his fellow representatives to have faith in the 'internal essence' of their community and in its ability to secure continued 'organic growth', even under changed circumstances.[24] Ultimately, members of the assembled *Kulturrat* took the plunge and voted unanimously to adopt cultural autonomy.

The decision opened the way to the formal election of a five-member cultural government (*Kulturverwaltung*) as the executive arm of autonomy. This comprised a series of administrative departments, reflecting its principal areas of activity, namely, education, culture, sport and youth affairs, and finance. A permanent secretariat was also set up, responsible, among other things, for supervision of the cultural curatoria (*Kulturkuratorium*) established in each of the nine electoral constituencies outside Tallinn in order to oversee the operation of cultural autonomy at the local level.[25] Housed in a handsome building with its own courtyard on Kohtu Street, close to the seat of government on Toompea, the physical location of the German cultural government underlined the fact that it was working on behalf of the state rather than in opposition to it. Nevertheless, the operation of cultural self-government entailed complex interactions with key ministries as well as local authorities, which inevitably took time to work out in practice.

Figure 4.1 The building housing the Baltic German Cultural Self-Government in Estonia.

The immediate priority of the cultural government was to ensure that every German child in Estonia had the opportunity to receive a formal education in his or her mother tongue within a coherent and unified network of German schools. Ideally, both private and public schools were to be included and would offer free elementary education to all pupils.[26] Estonia's existing law on primary schooling already obliged local authorities to provide education in the mother tongue wherever there were 20 school-age children belonging to a particular linguistic minority who could be taught by one teacher. Depending on numbers, minority-language education took place either in separate schools or in dedicated classes based within existing institutions.[27] Only in three locations – Tallinn, Tartu and Mustjas, close to Võru – were Germans sufficiently numerous to be guaranteed automatic access to state-funded schooling. The six public schools in these towns accounted for 36 per cent of the 3,739 pupils receiving German-language education in Estonia as of 1925. The remainder were in private schools (19 in total by 1925), funded by voluntary contributions from within the German community (under the terms of the so-called *Schulhilfe*) and augmented by official subsidies from Germany and by school fees. Nevertheless, private German-language schools remained chronically underfunded during the early post-independence years, despite charging high fees in many cases.[28]

The introduction of cultural autonomy now offered at last the possibility for the rationalization of German education under the auspices of the cultural government. The transfer of private German-language schools to its jurisdiction was relatively unproblematic, and took place at the start of 1926. However, when it came to handing over control of publicly funded schools, local authorities in Tallinn, Tartu and Mustjas proved reluctant to maintain the levels of financial support hitherto provided for these institutions. Moreover, the German cultural government had assumed that funding would be calculated on the basis of the number of pupils enrolled in individual schools. Tallinn city council, on the other hand, insisted that the proportion of the education budget falling to German-minority schools had to be worked out not on the basis of pupil numbers, but rather according to the ratio between those Germans enrolled on the national register and the overall population of the city. This obviously threatened to reduce the number of publicly funded classes for the German minority.[29] Although Estonia's ministry of education formally handed over control of publicly funded German-language schools to the cultural government at the start of the 1926–1927 school year, the local authorities concerned had still failed to agree on the amount of funds to be allocated by the required deadline of December 1926.[30]

Against this background the German cultural government faced an uphill struggle in its effort to reduce its costs by bringing some of the German-language private schools into the public sector. Not until 1928 was there any real resolution of issues surrounding public funding for German-language schools. Continued private contributions and increased cultural subsidies from Germany helped to cover any shortfall. Most significantly, however, the onset of cultural autonomy enabled the cultural government to supplement state support through the introduction of a system of self-taxation. This involved a compulsory levy on all adult members of the national register who were in employment. Defaulters were to be liable to legal action, enforced by the state. The tax, which was graduated according to income tax category, was to be fixed annually by the German cultural council.[31] As was the case with the upkeep of the national register, the actual collection of taxes was handled at the local and regional level by the *curatoria*. These filed tax returns to the central organs of cultural autonomy and had to account for non-payment on the part of individuals. Logically, the local bodies also dealt with requests for exemption from or reduction of the tax burden.[32]

A minute of the German cultural council from November 1927 indicates that evasion rates were relatively low, with 84 per cent of the tax having been collected on time. Overall, figures for 1926–1930 showed three successive annual rises in the amount of tax collected, followed by only a modest decline.[33] Werner Hasselblatt's perception in May 1928 that there had not been significant defections from the national register simply in order to avoid paying tax was thereby confirmed.[34] A later annual report for 1929 by the head of the cultural government recorded only 321 removals from the adult register during that year. Of these, 232 were due to deaths and there were only 89 cases of people actively requesting to be struck from the list. In the same period there were 416 new entrants. Adults signing up for the first time numbered 163. The remainder transferred from the youth register, having reached the age of eighteen. Overall, therefore, there had been an increase of 95 persons during the year, suggesting broad acceptance of the structures built since 1925.[35]

The success of a system that was ultimately founded on personal choice contrasts markedly with the approach to cultural taxation adopted under the 1920 Jewish autonomy law in Lithuania, which did not allow for opt-outs. As a result, taxation became a huge source of collective dissatisfaction and evasion was widespread. The resultant tensions within local Jewish communities made it even harder for leaders to maintain autonomy in the increasingly nationalistic atmosphere of early 1920s Lithuania.[36] Interestingly enough in parenthesis, this lesson appears to have been lost on Werner Hasselblatt who personally remained wedded to the coercive approach when it came to self-taxation, the chief secure source of income for cultural self-government.[37]

Once a comparatively firm financial base had been secured, the German cultural government could begin the practical task of constructing a single, integrated German school network. A unified system of management for all schools under the auspices of the cultural government allowed for immediate financial rationalization, producing an annual saving of up to half a million Estonian marks. In several cases, small rural elementary classes were now merged into a single unit (*Klassenkomplex*) for group teaching.[38] Elsewhere, however, funding was now also available to support new elementary schools in Elwa, Kersell, Sangla and Eidapere, as well as the expansion of boarding facilities at existing German-language schools. In addition, small grants could now be provided to enable children from remote areas to attend German-language schools.[39]

Supplementary funding continued to come from private sources even after the introduction of compulsory taxation. One prominent organization involved in this was the Union of German Associations *(Bund der deutschen Vereine)*.[40] Another private initiative was the establishment of a separate German girls' school in Tartu, managed and partly funded through the efforts of a locally formed organization. The cultural government on the whole welcomed such initiatives, providing they did not undermine its overall control of the direction and content of schooling. Inevitably, the formation of a German school network was accompanied by extensive and sometimes acrimonious debates over the nature and balance of educational provision.

Ewald Ammende might well have spoken of the need for German schools to teach 'in a German spirit'.[41] What this meant in practice, however, was less than clear. Did it imply retaining the classical gymnasium route leading to higher education and the professions? Or would the loss of Baltic Germans' privileged status put a premium on more practical and technical forms of education, thereby enabling school leavers more readily to hold their own within the society of independent Estonia? This was one of the central questions dividing the Baltic German community. On the one hand, German parents' associations had already been complaining for some time that there were too many secondary schools of the traditional type and that more emphasis should be placed on developing technical education.[42] Their objection was in turn contested after November 1925 by influential voices within the German cultural council who saw the gymnasium as the best way of preserving the German language and the sense of Germandom.[43] Inevitably, however, the wider debate over principles could hardly be divorced from practical questions of cost, notably, for example, the need to increase salaries in order to attract the best-qualified teachers. Long-term financial stability therefore required continuous monitoring of the school network as it evolved.

Remarkably, none of these problems prevented the emergence of a unified school network by the start of the 1927–1928 academic year. Its financial base was further consolidated in the course of 1928 through the transfer of 27 private German-language classes into the public school system.[44] With these developments came the capacity to offer free elementary education to all German-language pupils. Private schools forming part of the network provided the first four years of schooling free of charge to pupils whose parents were enrolled on the national register. In place of the fee income thus forfeited, private schools received an equivalent sum in the form of subventions from the cultural government. The cultural government also determined the level of the fees that became payable when pupils entered the fifth year of private schooling. At that point, parents enrolled on the national register paid reduced fees, although the same benefits could be enjoyed by non-members who made a contribution equivalent to the appropriate rate of cultural self-taxation.[45]

A report from 1928 suggests that even after payment of taxes to the cultural government was taken into account, parents who belonged to the national register still made an overall financial saving under this system.[46] Prior to the abolition of fees for elementary schooling, the cost of educating a child over 11 years stood at 68,000 Estonian marks. Following the rationalization under cultural government auspices, the amount fell to only 55,200 marks – a saving of 12,800 marks. The overall annual saving for German schooling was estimated at between one and two million marks.[47]

For all this, German cultural self-government found itself under significantly increased financial pressure by the turn of the decade. A major factor was the declining birth rate in Estonia during and after the First World War. The attendant generalized fall in primary and secondary school enrolment brought with it cuts in both state funding and fee income. How serious this was could be seen from the 1930–1931 budget of the cultural government, which, despite a 12 per cent reduction in equipment and teaching aids, was still showing a probable deficit of some 11,000 Estonian crowns.[48]

The shortfall in income inevitably meant that some sacrifices would have to be made in order to maintain the integrity of the school network. One interesting illustration of the tensions at the heart of autonomous schooling is provided by an ongoing dispute between the cultural government and Alfred Walter, director of the private German gymnasium in Tartu. Walter had opened primary classes in his school without the approval of the cultural government, which naturally saw these classes as a potential rival to the German-language public primary school in the town. Wilhelm von Wrangell, who took over from Harry Koch as head of the cultural government in 1932 following the latter's illness, conceded that his organization had no formal legal right to ban these classes. He nevertheless insisted that 'a common school policy, which is vital in the present difficult time, is only possible if individual groups heed the will of the cultural council even when there is no legal obligation to do so'.[49]

As it became apparent that a still more fundamental restructuring of the school network could no longer be delayed, the unity of the German minority was to be tested further over the coming year. The budgetary proposals put by the cultural government to the cultural council on 23 November 1930 envisaged no change to existing arrangements for Tallinn, but called for cuts to secondary school provision in Tartu, Fellin, Narva and Weissenstein. The alternative – maintaining the status quo – would have meant significant increases in cultural taxation for an already overstretched German community, something that the cultural council ruled unacceptable.[50]

The cultural council eventually gave its broad assent to the proposed budgetary cuts albeit with some modifications, such as the proviso that those secondary classes under threat could continue to operate if additional funding could be secured from elsewhere. Inevitably, however, where issues continued to arise about the extent and nature of schooling provision, there was still controversy. This in turn brought into focus widespread dissatisfaction within the German community regarding the procedures for electing the cultural council. The previous elections of 1925 and 1928 had provoked much criticism among voters in Tallinn and Tartu, the two towns accounting for three-quarters of the total German electorate. Many objected to the similarity of too many of the lists and the restrictions this placed upon voter choice. There was also a widespread perception that the electoral process itself was far too complex.[51]

As a result, Wilhelm von Wrangell, at that time still vice president of the German cultural government, prepared draft proposals addressing both issues. Essentially, he envisaged longer combined lists in which each competing group within the German community included all of its candidates. In order to counter local patriotism and to emphasize that the elections were about advancing the interests of the German community as a whole, candidates could appear on several lists and in several electoral districts, rather than being confined to a specific locality.[52]

The principle was broadly agreed, with some modifications based on a draft by Dr H. von Zedelmann from Tartu. This retained the principle of drawing up longer electoral lists, while also allowing electors to give supplementary votes to three favoured candidates (two in the case of smaller districts). Subsequently, every basic vote for each candidate plus every supplementary vote would be allocated to the list on which he/she stood. The candidates within the list were to be ranked according to the number of votes received, and the seats distributed to the various lists on the basis of the total share of the vote received by each. The *Revalsche Zeitung* optimistically reported that this draft struck a suitable balance between local concerns and the overall needs of the German minority.[53]

Another major aim in bringing German-language public and private schools into a single network had been to achieve broad control over issues such as staff selection, school inspections and curriculum development, which German representatives had previously highlighted as essential to the preservation of German cultural identity. For instance, it was noted that prior to the introduction of cultural autonomy, the 1,300 German-language pupils studying in Estonian public schools (more than one-third of the total) had not had the benefits of a link to any 'cultural organization of our people'.[54]

The report books of the German schools inspectorate certainly indicate that inculcating a 'German spirit', to use Ewald Ammende's phrase, was by no means always an easy matter, even after autonomy had been introduced. When school counsellor Emil Musso inspected the Walter school in Tartu on 12 December 1928, pupils told him that one of the teachers, Mr Lepp, listed Estonia's internal enemies as: 1. Communists, 2. Russian monarchists, and 3. Baltic Germans. Musso planned to raise this matter with Lepp at a second lesson due to take place on Wednesday 12 December. However, Lepp failed to attend, having submitted a doctor's note saying he was ill. Both Walter and Musso confirmed with the pupils that the remark had indeed been made, and then visited Lepp at his home in the afternoon. The latter admitted making the comment, but claimed he was acting according to an instruction containing materials which he used as the basis for his teaching.[55]

In his annual report for 1927, Johannes Beermann, now secretary to the cultural council, had also alluded to continued gripes within the German community over what was perceived as a lack of genuine autonomy due to excessive regulation by the ministry of education.[56] In Beermann's view, this was because initial expectations had been too high, with many regarding cultural autonomy as a sort of magic wand making anything possible. Second, the term cultural autonomy had confused people who overlooked the fact that 'we received self-government on the same basis as [existing] local authorities, in no way full autonomy, that is to say an administration completely independent of the state'.[57]

As suggested in the previous chapter, German minority control over the structure and content of schooling proved in practice to be more comprehensive in neighbouring Latvia during the late 1920s, albeit by dint of considerable effort by, and despite comparable misgivings within, the community. Admittedly, the prospect of a general autonomy law for Latvia's minorities had all but vanished by the end of 1925, and with it any chance of constituting a national minority as a public corporation. Instead, from 1923, Latvia's Germans made use of the *Zentrale deutschbaltischer Arbeit* through which they were able to introduce a system of voluntary self-taxation in 1926. The arrangement helped to consolidate the advances in German-language education already made on the basis of the 1919 law on minority schooling. With the exception of one ill-disposed incumbent during 1923, successive education ministers in Latvia had refrained from undue direct interference in the running of German schools. Such was certainly the view of Wolfgang Wachtsmuth, who headed the German school authority in the Latvian ministry of education from 1928 until 1934.[58]

Under both the Estonian and the Latvian systems, national minorities were defined on the basis of language. While this was on the whole unproblematic for Baltic Germans, it was much less so in the case of the Jewish minority for which language remained a major bone of political contention throughout the 1920s. In Latvia the terms of the 1919 education law at least partly mitigated linguistically based conflicts: the fact that the state arranged schooling on the basis of declared family language opened up the possibility of offering classes in both Yiddish and Hebrew. Despite ongoing disputes between the Yiddish and Hebrew camps, both languages were ultimately accommodated within the Jewish section of the ministry of education. Although Yiddish remained the predominant language of instruction, Latvia's only socialist government of the democratic era granted parity to both languages during 1926.[59]

Many Jewish pupils undergoing schooling in German and – especially – Russian initially came under other arrangements. In February 1920, Jacob Landau, head of the Jewish section within Latvia's ministry of education, noted that in some of the schools belonging to other minority sections no fewer than 90 per cent of the pupils were of Jewish origin.[60] Data from the Russian section of the ministry in the mid-1920s confirms that of 2,159 studying at 16 private Russian-language secondary schools, some 1,318 were of Jewish origin. Indeed, only 390 were Russian by nationality. The Jewish presence within private Russian-language elementary schools was even more striking.[61] On this basis, Jewish education officials within the ministry demanded at the very least a consultative role in the running of the schools in question, which were expected to incorporate the study of Hebrew and of Jewish history and culture into their curriculum.[62]

Zionist political forces within the council of the Jewish section had a more radical agenda, arguing that such schools should also be required to increase significantly the number of hours devoted to Jewish religion and culture at the expense of Russian grammar, history and literature. Furthermore, this was envisaged as a purely temporary expedient, pending the formal transfer of the schools to the Jewish section and a long-term shift towards a unified Jewish school system teaching in a 'single national language' – Hebrew.[63] Section head Jacob Landau, however, was wary of agitating for a transfer of schools from the Russian to the Jewish section. Citing the 'imprecise nature' of the 1919 law on minority schooling, he was concerned that the ministry might not take the Jewish side in this matter. Were it to rule that the affiliation of a school ought to be a question for the owner or for the school council, then the Jewish section might lose any possibility of exerting influence over those schools that were of most interest to it.[64]

In the course of his remarks Landau also reminded his colleagues that the language of instruction in particular schools was a matter for parents and children who were free to determine their own family language under the terms of the 1919 legislation. Following the line of the National Democratic Party to which he belonged, Landau also argued that it was simply not practical to contemplate a system of Jewish education delivered entirely in Hebrew. While underlining his commitment to promoting Jewish national identity, Landau nevertheless insisted that cultural advancement was also contingent on the material well-being of the community. Hitherto, Jewish families had habitually sent their children to Russian-language schools not because they considered Russian to be their 'national' language, but so as to give the pupil better opportunities to attend university or find work in Russia. Any attempt to abolish or even limit further the teaching of Russian (or other languages) in Jewish schools would simply result in a loss of pupils. As long as every Jewish child could be taught 'Jewish subjects', this would be more than sufficient to forestall the risk of 'denationalization'.[65]

Landau's National Democratic Party never again won seats in parliament after Latvia's first *Saiema*. Nevertheless he was able to retain his position as head of the Jewish section right through to

1934, despite pressure from within those circles advocating greater use of Hebrew and Yiddish in Jewish schools. Landau's longevity in office was due in no small part to the endorsement of Mordechai Dubin, Latvia's most influential Jewish politician, whose *Agudat Israel* party opposed the Zionist project of transforming the old Jewish liturgical language into a modern vernacular. As a conservative religious party, *Agudat* also voted consistently with Latvia's (mainly Agrarian Party-led) right-of-centre ruling coalitions during the years 1922–1934.[66]

Efforts by the Jewish education section to bring all Jewish pupils within its ambit were finally rewarded in the mid-1920s when the Russian section of the education ministry reversed its previous opposition and consented to the transfer of the disputed schools under its jurisdiction (see below). This decision appears consistent with a new line on national affiliation emanating from the education ministry, which issued a directive stating that all schools in which 60 per cent of pupils belonged to a particular minority (in this case, the Jewish) should come under the appropriate national authority.[67]

Progress towards the consolidation of a Jewish minority identity was also discernible at that time in neighbouring Estonia where the small Jewish community followed the German lead by electing its own 27-member cultural council in May 1926. This duly voted in favour of implementing cultural autonomy and appointed a cultural government consisting of seven members, as well as establishing local *curatoria* in Tartu, Narva, Pärnu, Rakvere, Viljandi and Valga.[68] What followed during the course of the next few years has been described as a form of Jewish national awakening, evidenced by the establishment of new schools and a plethora of clubs and societies. Tallinn's existing Jewish school was quickly integrated into the state network and a new secondary school set up in Tartu (1926) and a new primary school in Valga (1928).[69] Between 1923 and 1935 the proportion of Jewish students studying in Jewish schools rose from 33 to 56 per cent.[70]

Such advances did not prevent continued debate within the Jewish cultural council among different political groupings, further underlining the complexity of defining Jewish identity and raising additional thorny questions concerning the respective jurisdictions of minority cultural self-governments on the one hand and, on the other, Estonia's existing local authorities. One of the

Jewish cultural council's first rulings was that teaching at the Jewish school in Tallinn should be in Hebrew. Although this decision reflected majority opinion within the cultural council, it nevertheless proved controversial amongst the wider Jewish public.[71] Continued demands for Yiddish-language education coming from the Jewish population in the capital ultimately prompted the creation of a separate private school, which the cultural government refused to incorporate into the new autonomous Jewish school network.

In a letter to Estonia's education ministry in September 1926 the Tallinn local educational authority (*koolivalitsus*) also noted that several Jewish parents had requested permission to send their children to a non-Jewish school on the grounds that no one in the family spoke Hebrew, only Yiddish, Russian or German.[72] A full 12 months later the ministry sent a reply confirming that a child who did not speak Hebrew at home could not be compelled to attend a Hebrew-language school. Citing the law on primary schooling, the ministry ruled that the children in question were entitled to receive education at home or at a school teaching in another language. In this case, moreover, the choice of school was entirely down to the parents: the permission of the local educational authority was required only where the district already contained a school teaching in the relevant mother tongue.[73]

The Jewish cultural government objected strongly to this ruling, insisting on its sole right to decide whether Jewish parents be allowed to send their children to a non-Jewish school. The same law on education also stipulated that the mother tongue of a child was to be determined according to his or her nationality. On this basis the Jewish authorities argued somewhat disingenuously that the national language had to be considered the mother tongue. Since Hebrew and Yiddish were both Jewish national languages, it followed that the Hebrew-language primary school had the status of a mother-tongue school. Therefore, all Jewish children were obliged to study in it unless the Jewish cultural government decided otherwise.[74]

After further deliberation, Estonia's ministry of education came round to the viewpoint of the Jewish cultural government. In a later exchange of correspondence with the Tallinn local educational authority in June and July 1928, it was stated that under the terms of the law on cultural self-government, local authorities no longer had any obligations towards members of national minorities as far as educational matters were concerned. Henceforth, in cases where a child belonged to a minority group that had opted for cultural autonomy, permission to study in a non-native language school could only be granted by the relevant minority self-government.[75]

The requirement to seek such permission did not, however, apply to those parents of Jewish nationality who were not enrolled on the national register. Faced with the new regulations, many Jewish parents who had initially opted for membership simply struck their names from the list and sought to place their children in non-Jewish schools. The Jewish cultural government then maintained that for local education authorities to accede to these demands would threaten the very existence of Jewish education in Estonia, given the small numbers of pupils involved. The Russification or Germanization of the Jewish minority, it argued, did not conform to the principles of a healthy state and nationalities policy. For reasons of state prestige (Estonia having been the first country to give its minorities cultural autonomy), the Jewish cultural government should have the sole right to grant permission to study in non-Jewish schools, regardless of whether or not a person belonged to the Jewish national register. The ministry of education, however, ruled quite correctly that this would contradict the terms and guiding principles of the 1925 autonomy law.[76]

If the German and Jewish minorities of Estonia and Latvia exhibited different profiles and preoccupations during the 1920s, the degree of dissimilarity between these two groups on the one hand and, on the other, the local Russian population was even more striking. By far the largest of the minority nationalities in interwar Estonia and Latvia, ethnic Russians also presented the biggest challenges in terms of societal integration. In both countries the Russian minority was predominantly rural, poor and illiterate, concentrated mainly in eastern border districts that had for the most part never belonged to the pre-war Baltic provinces and were thus only incorporated into Estonia and Latvia as a result of the 1920 peace treaties with Soviet Russia. The communal system of agriculture inherited from the Tsarist period was gradually abolished in the course of the 1920s, but most local residents were left to eke out a living on small rented plots of land in areas where birth rates and population density remained significantly higher than the national average. Land hunger was compounded by the loss of traditional markets in the Russian hinterland, not least for the long-established Russian fishing communities on the western shores of Lake Peipsi in Estonia.[77]

As far as cultural recognition was concerned, the compactly settled Russian population of eastern Estonia was able to utilize the territorially based provisions for minority rights established under the 1918 school law and the constitution of 1920. By the end of the first decade of independence there were over 100 Russian-language primary schools in Estonia, with over 9,000 pupils. A further 1,000 were studying in Russian-language secondary schools.[78] The progress made in developing Russian-language education during these years owed much to the work of Aleksei Janson, who served as Russian national secretary within Estonia's ministry of education from 1922 to 1927. In 1923, Janson also helped to establish the Union of Russian Educational and Charitable Societies, which he chaired for the first four years of its existence.[79]

A man of both cultures – Estonian and Russian – and a tireless champion of minority cultural rights in Russia during the last years of Tsarist rule, Janson was also a committed socialist. For him, developing Russian-language school-age and adult education was central to improving the economic lot of the rural Russian population and to integrating the eastern borderlands more thoroughly into the new framework of the Republic of Estonia. Quickly disillusioned by what he saw as the state's lack of support for these areas, he urged local Russians to organize themselves more effectively in order to maximize their political influence.[80]

Janson's call for the establishment of Russian cultural autonomy was echoed by elements of the right-of-centre Russian National Union (RNU) founded in Estonia during 1920. While describing the existing educational provisions for the Russian minority as the most generous in Europe, commentators from within RNU still alluded to 'unwanted difficulties' that could sometimes arise in a system that remained wholly under the auspices of central state government.[81] Full cultural autonomy, it was argued, would give Russian representatives a far greater say in areas such as staff recruitment and curriculum design, while allowing the Russian minority to claim a larger share of the cultural funding disbursed by the Estonian state.

The most prominent exponent of this view was the Tartu University professor and RNU politician Mikhail Kurchinskii, whose previous research on municipal government and finances left him well placed to grapple with the complexities of the 1925 law on cultural autonomy. With a network of state-administered Russian-language schools already in place many local Russian commentators baulked at an autonomy scheme that would entail the payment of additional taxes to a Russian cultural self-government. By contrast, in a series of articles published during the late 1920s and early 1930s, Kurchinskii emphatically denied that autonomy would impose an undue financial burden for the already straitened Russian community. According to his calculations, fully 65 per cent of the 325,000 Estonian Crowns spent annually by the German cultural self-government came from state and municipal subsidies, and only 75,000 from cultural taxation. If 18,000 Germans could collect this sum, argued Kurchinskii, surely 90,000 Russians could do the same? With a progressive system of taxation, less well-off members of the community would be required to contribute less than one crown per year, far below, he claimed, what the average person spent annually on vodka![82]

While the size of the Russian minority could be construed as advantageous in terms of implementing cultural autonomy, it also

Figure 4.2 Professor Mikhail Kurchinskii.

presented considerable practical obstacles. Registering 12,000 Germans in the course of 1925 had been a significant feat even for a community that was largely urban and comparatively socially cohesive. Russian advocates of cultural autonomy would have been required to garner some three times that number and this from amongst a population that displayed high levels of illiteracy as well as living mostly in isolated rural settlements.[83] In the political context of the late 1920s and early 1930s, Kurchinskii's carefully crafted rational arguments in favour of autonomy failed to carry the Russian elite. In the view of his detractors, the Tartu academic was insufficiently versed in the realities of a rural Russian 'periphery' that had little interest in secondary schooling and was content to leave responsibility for primary education in the hands of central government.[84]

Kurchinskii did in fact come to appreciate the scale of these obstacles. He nonetheless continued to insist that the preparatory work to establish cultural autonomy would in itself serve as a 'sociopolitical school' for a Russian population that could hardly be described as 'a single united national whole'.[85] In his view, the main barrier to autonomy lay in the existence of a host of 'mutually antagonistic ... organizations', many of which feared a loss of influence should control of Russian cultural affairs pass to a single elected self-government body.[86] Here, Kurchinskii was obviously referring first and foremost to the Union of Russian Educational and Charitable Societies headed by his bitter political rival Aleksei Janson.

The Russian population in Latvia was similarly beset by political divisions, and this state of affairs ultimately proved detrimental not just to specifically Russian interests, but also to the political influence of Latvia's minorities as a whole. The National Democratic Union of Russian Citizens of Latvia (NDU), formed prior to Latvia's independence, actively discussed a law on Russian national–cultural autonomy during the early 1920s, but its endeavours were undermined by the failure of Russians to unite and cooperate effectively.[87] The NDU quickly lost any pretensions as a broad-based national organization, splitting into a liberal democratic nationalist fraction (*Russkoe Obshchestvo v Latvii*), which advocated close cooperation with all national groups inhabiting Latvia, and a more rightist nationalist grouping (the Russian National Union) adhering to the principles of ethnic exclusivity.[88] It can only be presumed that the latter tendency concurred with the July 1925 ministry of education ruling on those Russian-language schools with a preponderance of Jewish pupils, paving the way for the transfer of ten private Russian-language schools to the Jewish minority section. Even so, the action elicited vigorous debates amongst Russian officials within the ministry.[89]

There were also divisions between the mainly urban-based Russian leadership in western Latvia and representatives from rural Latgale, where a significant minority of Russian-speaking inhabitants were also religious Old Believers and thus adhered to their own specific cultural practices. Latgalian representatives such as *Saiema* deputy MA Kallistratov complained that the views and concerns of his constituents were insufficiently represented within the Russian section of Latvia's education ministry.[90]

Russian organizations at least briefly managed to set aside their differences, uniting behind the candidacy of Professor I. F. Yupatov, who in December 1923 was appointed head of the Russian section within the education ministry.[91] As noted earlier, the National Democratic Union also initiated discussions on a draft cultural autonomy law for the Russian minority, but such efforts were undermined by in-fighting between the various Russian parties and factions represented in parliament, as well as by a failure to cooperate effectively with representatives of other minority groups. By November 1926, the Russian parliamentary faction had collapsed, and with it the entire minority bloc within the *Saiema*.[92]

Advocates of Russian cultural autonomy could nevertheless draw comfort from the fact that nine out of ten ethnic Russian children in Latvia were receiving primary education in their native language by the end of the 1920s.[93] This was despite the covert agenda pursued from 1924 by a secret committee of bureaucrat nationalists, drawn from the key departments of central government. This body was committed to nationalizing the eastern borderlands of Latvia by drawing non-ethnically Latvian pupils out of minority-language schools and into those teaching in Latvian.

As part of this strategy, Latvian-language primary schools received extra funding towards the provision of free school meals, a major enticement for poor rural families in particular. Whereas schools controlled by the German and Jewish sections were able to compete in the lunch stakes by raising additional private funding, Russian-language schools were considerably more vulnerable in this regard.[94] Such illegal practices during the 1920s once again demonstrate how choice of nationality or language of schooling were not always determined solely by the personal preference of the individual, but were contingent on a whole range of constraints and incentives. In the final analysis, however, the lunch initiative does not appear to have met with great success, given the proportion of Russian-language pupils still attending Russian schools at the end of the decade.

In a more general review of a decade of autonomous schooling in Latvia, the outgoing head of the German education authority, Karl Keller, reported in 1929 that irrespective of political differences between the political parties and some hostility from sections of the Latvian press, the idea of a minority having its own cultural existence had been recognized as being to the general good.[95] Keller recalled the initial strong resistance among officials and the wider public, which he ascribed partly to the legacy of a Tsarist state alien to the concept of free national development. Ultimately, however, the early clashes between minority representatives and the bureaucracy over aspects of the legislation had given way to a situation where autonomous schooling was accepted in official circles and was gaining support from public opinion, albeit sometimes as a necessary evil. In this respect, what seemed to bother Latvians, as it plainly did many Estonians, was the idea that minority schools might be superior to those catering for the ethnic majority. Keller found it difficult to assess the response of the mass of Latvians, but believed that difficulties in setting up new minority schools reflected concern about the likely fiscal burden to the local authority rather than hostility towards the idea as such.[96]

German officials in Estonia were similarly encouraged by the initial experience of cultural autonomy during the late 1920s. In his final report to the first German cultural council in 1928, Harry Koch claimed that despite continuing difficulties and uncertainties the risk had been well worth taking.[97] His understanding seems to have been shared by other observers at the turn of the 1930s, who claimed that earlier fears of autonomy giving rise to states within states had now been conclusively dispelled. *Revaler Bote* editor Axel de Vries, for instance, in reviewing the previous five years recorded a positive view of cultural autonomy (now embracing '100 per cent of Germans'), despite shortcomings arising from the framework nature of the 1925 law.[98] His view was shared by

Eugen Madisson, one of the key Estonian state officials who oversaw autonomy, as well as by no less a figure than Social Democrat Party leader Mikhel Martna, who had been one of the most vociferous opponents of cultural autonomy in the parliamentary debates of the early 1920s.[99]

These upbeat assessments of the first post-independence decade, however, mask the continued resentment voiced by more nationalizing circles unhappy at the disproportionate influence of both Germans and Jews within the urban economy. Claims of integration through cultural autonomy are also hard to sustain in the case of the Russian minorities living in Latvia and Estonia, who remained marginalized within the new socio-economic order. Contemporary accounts on the pages of the Riga-based Russian-language daily *Segodniia* suggested that ethnicity remained the primary basis for self-identification amongst local Russians who also continued to view themselves as part of a broader, transnational cultural community. A decade on from independence, only 15 per cent of Latvia's Russians were conversant with Latvian, whereas Germans and Jews (along with half of ethnic Latvians) were usually able to speak two, three or even four languages.[100]

While this trend was not in itself immediately threatening to the integrity of the Latvian state, the failure to improve economic conditions in Latgale – home to three-quarters of Latvia's Russians as well as to an ethnically Belorussian population – increased the potential allure of propaganda from the neighbouring USSR. Aleksei Janson voiced similar concerns with regard to the eastern districts of neighbouring Estonia, claiming in 1925 that 'here, unlike in Soviet Russia, dreams of a socialist paradise remain very much alive'.[101]

The likes of Paul Schiemann and Mikhail Kurchinskii often reminded their ethnic compatriots in Latvia and Estonia of how favoured their situation was in comparison with that of German and Russian minorities elsewhere. Both politicians, however, also appreciated that the progress made in their own countries could be best secured in the long term by extending the campaign for cultural autonomy beyond the Baltic states to the wider European arena. Only through simultaneous work at this level, they reasoned, could the construction of prosperous and integrated state communities be guaranteed.

5 Nationalities in congress

In a letter to the editor of the *Frankfurter Zeitung* on 25 February 1925, Ewald Ammende hailed the adoption of Estonia's cultural autonomy law as 'an important achievement for all minorities and a decisive step towards national rapprochement'.[1] Understandably, there was much satisfaction on the part of Ammende, Schiemann, Kurchinskii and other minority activists with the way in which fears of cultural autonomy as a harbinger of states within states had been greatly reduced, at least within their own Baltic homelands. Taking this message beyond the borders of their respective countries, however, presented a more formidable challenge.

In the first instance it meant having to convince the League of Nations of the benefits of cultural autonomy for the protection of all national minorities in Europe. Minority leaders were by now thoroughly disillusioned with the opaque and ineffective procedures put in place by the League. In a newspaper interview in Geneva on 4 September 1926, Schiemann poured scorn on the 'senseless remarks' of the League rapporteur Afranio Mello Franco, whom he charged with having 'no idea at all' of the European situation. Franco's view, he added, may have been unduly influenced by his Brazilian background and the very different set of issues pertaining to immigration in South America.[2] Two years later, Schiemann reiterated his dismay by attacking the way in which League committees were 'swallowing' minority petitions. In this 'shocking act' he saw a cynical 'reduction of the will to peace to lip service to peace'.[3]

By the mid-1920s, German minority leaders had already accumulated considerable experience in organizing themselves across borders through the *Verband der deutschen Minderheiten in*

Figure 5.1 Afranio Mello Franco.

Europa. To reiterate, the proclaimed mission of the *Verband* was, first, to counter the prevailing sense of isolation and helplessness amongst the scattered German communities of Eastern Europe. A second objective was to campaign for cultural autonomy, initially for German minorities, within Europe's existing borders. However, Ammende's travels in Europe had convinced him that the quest for cultural autonomy would be all the more effective if non-German minority representatives could be persuaded to make common cause with the *Verband* in forming a new European-wide organization. Doubtless, Ammende's search for a new area of activity was also at least partly due to his disappointment at not being offered the key post of secretary to the *Verband*. This had gone to Carl Georg Bruns, a respected Berlin-based specialist in international law. More to the point, Bruns had good connections to the German foreign office, whose financial support was essential to the *Verband*'s operation.[4]

Figure 5.2 Ewald Ammende.

Figure 5.3 Carl Bruns.

Ammende's initiative to reach out to non-German minorities also has to be seen in the context of the expectations aroused by German Foreign Minister Gustav Stresemann's endorsement of cultural autonomy for all European minorities in a memorandum of 13 January 1925 entitled 'The foreign policy imperative for a regulation of minorities' rights within the Reich corresponding to the needs of German minorities in Europe'. Stresemann's action was based on advice from Bruns following a period of intensive lobbying by German minority leaders. Their efforts had culminated in a Berlin conference in autumn 1924, which among other things afforded an opportunity for personal contact between German minority representatives and influential political figures in Germany. Further impetus was given by the prospect of Germany's entry to the League of Nations and along with it the opportunity for the Reich government to take the lead over minority issues in Europe.[5]

Stresemann's celebrated memorandum endorsing cultural autonomy certainly recognized the advantages to Germany in

Figure 5.4 Gustav Stresemann.

taking the lead in the quest for minority rights.[6] Yet it clearly
betrays the influence of the arguments coming from *Verband*
circles. Hostile critics have seized on Stresemann's oblique reference in his text to the 'distant goal' of 'creating a state whose
political borders embrace all German groups inhabiting the
compact German settlement areas in *Mitteleuropa* who wish to be
part of the Reich'.[7] However, at the heart of the document is an
extended defence of the need to establish a moral case for realizing this objective, one which by implication ruled out the use of
force. Not only that, but Stresemann insisted that Germany itself
set an example by according cultural autonomy to the national
minorities living within its own borders. In his own words:

> Recognizing the existence of a natural right of every national
> minority to cultural autonomy and above all to its own
> schooling, is at the heart of what has to be fought for on
> behalf of German minorities in Europe, and must therefore at
> the same time be central to what has to be allowed and unas-
> sailably guaranteed to the minorities in the *Reich*, before
> Germany can represent before the world this necessity of life.[8]

The wording of Stresemann's memorandum reflected his obvious
need to balance between different political factions inside
Germany. These divisions were replicated to a significant extent
within the ranks of the *Verband der deutschen Minderheiten*. For
Ewald Ammende a major consideration behind the campaign for
cultural autonomy was the need to counter Soviet propaganda
aimed at the disaffected minorities of central and Eastern Europe.[9]
He saw the reintegration of Germany into a united Western European bloc as the best means of doing so, acknowledging within
this the value of the League of Nations, however imperfect.
Werner Hasselblatt fully shared Ammende's loathing of Bolshevism, but at the same time viewed the West as inimical to the
interests of Germandom as a whole and as a barrier to the
increase of German influence within the international system.

Hassleblatt's thinking comes out very clearly in a draft document for the *Deutsch-Baltische Partei in Estland* (DBP) dating
from the turn of 1924–1925. Essentially, his argument rests on
the contention that neither East nor West could provide a lasting
solution to nationality issues. With regard to the East he argued
that although the Soviet Union acknowledged the power of

national sentiment by allowing nationalities to have their own schools, administration and use of their mother tongue, this was exploited solely for the purposes of communist ideology. Thus the approval of the national principle was accompanied by the destruction of the intelligentsia and the elimination of the leading bourgeois sectors.

Unlike Ammende, however, Hasselblatt saw no solution as coming from the West, either. In his view, the peacemakers had stirred up the nationalities movement, thereby initiating inter-state quarrels that could not be overcome between states, that is to say in the first instance through the League of Nations. From this he deduced that Germany, 'the heart of Europe', was best placed to take up the minorities issue and to create a new legal instrument which Germany would be better able to apply than its national opponents. This instrument was culturally autonomous self-government (*Kulturautonome Selbstverwaltung*).[10] To cut a long story short, all *Verband* members, if from vastly differing motives, were encouraged by Stresemann's initiative.

Arrangements duly went ahead for the first-ever truly European-wide meeting of minority leaders, scheduled to be held in October 1925. As early as February of that same year, Ammende had drafted his 'reasons, principles and programme for a conference of representatives of all national minorities in Europe'. This became the basis for exploratory talks over the months that followed, culminating in a so-called invitation conference in Dresden in August.[11] The venue for the new Congress of European Nationalities was to be Geneva, thereby taking advantage of the media circus that attended meetings of the League of Nations Council. On all but three occasions, subsequent annual meetings always took place in Geneva just ahead of the League Council sessions.[12]

The 50 delegates at the inaugural autumn 1925 conference were drawn from no fewer than 34 national groups belonging to 17 different states, mostly but not exclusively in central and Eastern Europe. During the life of the Congress, some 219 delegates took part in its annual meetings. Of these, Germans were the most numerous (74) and, together with Jewish representatives (25), made up just under half of the total membership. In terms of country of origin, as opposed to ethnicity, 51 delegates came from Poland, 29 each from Romania and Czechoslovakia, 23 from Spain, 13 from Germany, 12 each from Latvia and Yugoslavia, 11

Figure 5.5 European Nationalities Congress.

each from Estonia and Austria, nine each from Hungary and Italy, four from Lithuania, three from Bulgaria, and one each from Belgium and Denmark.[13]

The importance of the German element within the Congress was reflected in the make-up of its executive board and in Ewald Ammende's appointment as general secretary. It was, however, far from being what its critics have regarded as a purely German affair. The president of the Congress was the Slovene Josip Wilfan, formerly a deputy in the Italian parliament. Estonian Russian Mikhail Kurchinskii became vice-president from 1927. Furthermore, those German minority leaders that played the most prominent role in the early years of the Congress were on the liberal side of the political spectrum, the most notable example being Paul Schiemann. It was the non-German Wilfan who would later describe Schiemann as 'the thinker of the European minorities movement', thus implicitly placing him at the forefront of a transnational as opposed to purely German endeavour.[14]

In its initial resolutions of October 1925 the Nationalities Congress endorsed the League of Nations' position that equal political and economic rights must be given to all citizens of the states created or enlarged under the peace settlement, irrespective of nationality. For members of national minorities this included the right and the opportunity to learn the language of the ethnic majority, which the Nationalities Congress accepted would necessarily be in most instances the sole official vehicle for state business. At the same time, persons belonging to minority groups should have the right to education in their own language, as well as the possibility of using that language without restriction in private intercourse between citizens and in the religious sphere. In localities where minorities made up a predominant share of the population, the relevant minority language should have official status alongside that of the majority.[15] In the view of Congress members, however, these rights could only be fully guaranteed through a system of non-territorial cultural autonomy that accorded minority groups the status of public legal corporations with full control over education and culture. A resolution to this effect was adopted at the close of the first Congress meeting.

In endorsing a non-territorial approach to the question of autonomy, the Nationalities Congress pointedly signalled its commitment to working within the confines of Europe's present borders. When asked by a journalist why the Congress did not criticize the lawless actions of some European governments, its vice president Paul Schiemann stated emphatically that minority representatives had gathered in Geneva not to make protests, but to draw out general goals about how nationalities could live together in the future. Some actions, he admitted, made silence difficult: notably, Italy's attempt to make Germans living in Süd-Tyrol Italianize their names. The fact that Wilfan – himself a Slovene deputy in the Italian parliament – had urged the Congress not to respond aggressively to this provocation was, Schiemann stressed, further proof of the essential moderation that reigned within the new organization. When asked whether such moderation would bring about a change in the attitude of European governments, Schiemann glanced at Rudolf Brandsch, representative of the Siebenburger Germans, and both replied 'with a sigh' that they hoped so.[16]

The refusal to countenance any discussion of border disputes at Congress meetings, coupled with an explicit stipulation that delegates refrain from airing grievances against specific governments, was in itself a riposte to the attitudes expressed by officials within the League of Nations, many of whom had voiced some foreboding about the new international forum.[17] Clearly, the Congress stance was also intended to reduce anxiety amongst the new and reconstituted states of Eastern Europe, particularly Poland and its patron France. Naturally, Schiemann made clear, the Congress resolutions would be made available to the League of Nations Council. For the moment, however, the Congress was most concerned with influencing public opinion more widely within Europe.

Particularly energetic in this latter respect was the Congress general secretary Ewald Ammende. He recognized only too well just how much 'hard work' would be required if the Estonian model of cultural autonomy was to be extended to other areas.[18] In a battery of private letters sent to newspaper editors across Europe in the aftermath of the first Congress meeting, Ammende underlined the benefits for 'our [i.e. German minority] cause' that would accrue from having other minority groups on board. This, he asserted, would help to counter charges that the Nationalities Congress was a purely 'German machination'.[19] Ammende also pandered openly in his correspondence to rightist German elements, both within his own Baltic community and more broadly. Thus, in the matter of German-language press coverage, he asserted that the initiative had to be presented 'not as a democratic but rather a purely national affair'.[20] Although Ammende was based in Vienna with the support of a permanent Congress secretariat from 1927, he travelled continuously in between annual Congress meetings, lobbying leading figures in the field of nationality rights. In so doing, the Janus-faced general secretary frequently asserted that he was speaking not just for German minorities, but on behalf of no fewer than 40 million souls who fell into the category of national minority.[21]

Efforts to encourage European states to embrace cultural autonomy for their national minorities went hand in hand with an intensified drive to secure reform of the League of Nations minority protection procedures. One obvious way of giving minorities greater voice would have been to create a standing committee at the League, devoted exclusively to the affairs of national minorities. Such a proposition had already been advanced by the Inter-Parliamentary Union and the Union of League of Nations Societies, and was endorsed by the Nationalities Congress in 1928.[22] The advantage of such a standing committee was that it would remove decisions on appeals from the hands of the League Council, where state considerations too often prevailed. For this reason Nationalities Congress representatives continued to be particularly incensed by the likes of Mello Franco and the Greek representative Nikolaos Politis, whose statements appeared to shut off any prospect of general national rights developing from the minority treaties and instead implied the assimilation of minorities in the longer term.[23]

As anticipated, increased pressure for reform of minority protection procedures came with Germany's entry to the League of Nations in March 1926. Minority leaders took particular heart from Stresemann's actions at the Lugano meeting of the League Council in December 1928. Following a provocative remark by the Polish delegate Ksawery Zalewski about the situation in Upper Silesia, the German foreign minister angrily reminded the Council about the League's professed obligations towards minorities. His point, that for the League not to fulfil its duties in this respect would make it illusory, found broad acceptance from the audience. No less a figure than Aristide Briand admitted as much in his closing remarks. In that respect Paul Schiemann rightly argued that Stresemann's intervention at Lugano had 'brought the minorities question into play once more'.[24]

Indeed, the discussions at Lugano gave rise to a review of minority protection procedures and a series of suggested changes aimed at bringing greater transparency to the petitioning process. These were prepared by a League commission – chaired by Japan, but including Britain and Spain as members – which presented its findings to the Madrid meeting of the League Council on 12 June 1929. However, Stresemann's key demand, namely for a permanent minorities committee at the League, was refused, moving him to write an impassioned defence of his actions in the *Kölnische Volkszeitung* on 1 August 1929. Here, Stresemann accused his detractors of 'an insufficient or mistaken perception of the essence of the minorities question'.[25] For him, that question was not a matter of preferential treatment, but of equal treatment. He insisted that the issue could be only be properly understood if not seen in a vacuum, but in the context of overall political development. In what appears to be a strong echo of Schiemann's thinking, Stresemann concluded that 'this historically realized incongruence between state and nation cannot be ended by any drawing of boundaries'.[26]

Not surprisingly for Ammende and his colleagues in the Nationalities Congress, the Madrid episode confirmed beyond doubt that recourse to existing League mechanisms could not in itself bring about the psychological change that would be required on the part of state governments and majority nationalities if the Congress agenda was to be implemented.[27] The only feasible alternative was to concentrate all efforts upon improving majority–minority relations within states. At the 1931 meeting of the Nationalities Congress, Ammende and other colleagues from Estonia once again held up recent experiences in that country as an example worthy of emulation elsewhere. The past five years, it was claimed, had shown the fears previously voiced about cultural autonomy to be completely unfounded. Far from creating states within a state, German and Jewish cultural autonomy had actually contributed to a growing détente between titular and non-titular national groups. Rather than focusing solely on the negative aspects of the minorities question, the League, it was suggested, should examine Estonian cultural autonomy more thoroughly, with a view to ascertaining whether this model might indeed advantageously be applied elsewhere.[28]

In making these claims Ammende was at the very least glossing over some serious reservations that many representatives of European minorities had expressed with regard to the concept of non-territorial cultural autonomy. Resistance came in the first instance from Polish quarters. The Polish minority within Germany claimed to detect behind calls for cultural autonomy only the desire for the interests of Germany to be advanced. By way of evidence they cited the inclusion in the Nationalities Congress of those German groups still demanding border changes. Leading representatives of the Polish community in Germany, notably Jan Skala, launched an attack along these lines in the journal of the Association of Minorities in Germany, *Kulturwehr*.[29] His article prompted in turn a fierce defensive action by Schiemann and others in the pages of *Nation und Staat*, which as it happened became the official journal of the Nationalities Congress in 1931.

Schiemann freely acknowledged the presence of irredentist elements within the Nationalities Congress, but maintained that their inclusion was premised on their readiness to accept Congress rules and, therefore, to work towards a peaceful solution to nationality disputes which would ultimately remove the basis for irredentism. As he pointed out, had the Congress not tried to engage such activists, it would have had little prospect of realizing its larger goals. Schiemann also saw in the German–Polish dispute evidence of a key difference in approach to minority issues on the part of the two groups. What the Congress wanted, he insisted, was: first, the exclusion of border issues from the nationalities movement; second, the inclusion in the movement of all organized minorities with their own culture; finally, the creation of internationally acknowledged laws guaranteeing free national cultural development irrespective of which state national groups belonged to. By contrast, Schiemann maintained, the Polish-led Association of National Minorities in Germany was less interested in the pursuit of minority rights than it was in trying to enforce the existing provisions of the peace treaties and, therefore, to exclude those minorities – chiefly German – whom it considered a threat to the status quo. Damningly, from Schiemann's viewpoint, the Poles in Germany expected the state rather than minorities themselves to take responsibility for culture.[30]

Despite Schiemann's eloquent defence, the Association of National Minorities in Germany precipitated the first major crisis for the Nationalities Congress by withdrawing from it in 1927. The immediate pretext for this action was the refusal by the Congress leadership to admit the representatives of Germany's Friesian population. The Congress executive detected in the Polish championing of Friesian membership a calculated manoeuvre to fragment and weaken the organization by introducing what Schiemann termed 'pseudo minorities'.[31]

Notwithstanding the political motivations behind this episode, it raised several issues of principle related to cultural autonomy that the Nationalities Congress would never satisfactorily resolve over the next five years. Not least, the dispute highlighted the perennial difficulty of agreeing what actually constitutes a genuine national minority. The German group within the Congress stood firmly by its so-called Dresden Resolution which made recognition of minority status contingent upon a clear declaration of will by a majority of the group in question in those cases where history and practice had not already established the clear existence of such a minority. In this particular dispute it was held that to embrace the 14,000 German Friesians within the Congress, when 13,500 had 'expressly' made clear that they did not want to be considered as belonging to a national minority, would have been a 'slap in the face' for the minorities movement.

Pending a better definition of minority, the German group was reluctant to abandon its position.[32]

Renner and Bauer's view of a national minority as something constituted on the basis of free affiliation clearly favoured those national communities that could draw upon a high level of socio-political cohesion. A case in point was provided by Estonia's Germans, who were predominantly urban, highly educated and relatively well-off members of a former ruling elite.[33] Other national groups, however, could not realistically aspire to reach such a position and with it the economic base necessary to implement and sustain what were after all highly complex arrangements. This is illustrated not least by Mikhail Kurchinskii's aforementioned inability to persuade Estonia's Russians of the merits of embracing cultural autonomy.

The absence of the sort of collective national will of which Schiemann and others spoke was further highlighted by the lack of any effective Russian transnational association comparable to the *Verband der deutschen Minderheiten*. Despite the creation of a Russian Bureau in Geneva in 1927 it was not until August 1929, ahead of the fifth Nationalities Congress, that Kurchinskii and others were able to arrange a conference bringing together representatives of Europe's Russian minorities. Attending this were representatives from the six East European countries in which Russian minorities lived. The meeting adopted a declaration endorsing the Nationalities Congress line on the reform of League procedures and its call for cultural autonomy for all minority groups. It nevertheless brought to light deep divisions within the Russian camp.[34]

Mikhail Kurchinskii had particular cause to lament the refusal by Latvian Russian representatives to attend meetings of the Nationalities Congress. The fact that Russians living in Latvia were, relatively speaking, quite privileged when it came to minority rights, Kurchinskii pointed out, made their participation all the more important as an example to less advantaged minority groups. In response, the Russian representatives from Latvia expressed reservations about joining the Congress until such time as their own organization was sufficiently strong. Otherwise they feared being towed along by stronger national groups, German above all.[35] Talk of securing better representation for the seven-and-a-half-million-strong Russian minority in central and Eastern Europe also appeared to overlook the fact that a sizeable proportion of these 'Russians' were in fact ethnic Ukrainians, many of whom aspired to their own separate nationhood and who were already represented separately in the Nationalities Congress on this basis.[36]

Despite claims of a German–Slavic divide within the Congress, there were certain reservations regarding the practice of cultural autonomy that were shared to some extent by representatives of all minorities. One particular concern, already voiced in Estonia in 1925, related to the establishment of national registers and public corporations. Germans from Slesvig and Hungary were apparently amongst those who expressed fears that the public registration of nationality by individual citizens risked those citizens being branded as a caste apart and thereby made the object of differential treatment by the state.[37] Others suspected that the system might even undermine rather than enhance minority national identity by introducing dissension and legal differentiation within the group. As the Estonian case had already shown to some extent, these concerns were perhaps of greatest relevance for the Jewish minorities of central and Eastern Europe, where a plurality of cultural and political orientations and public opinion were especially apparent.

However much Ewald Ammende might wish these reservations away, they obviously undermined efforts by the Nationalities Congress to persuade the League of the Nations of the merits of non-territorial cultural autonomy. In a comprehensive analysis of the concept drafted in 1931, Ludvig Krabbe of the League Minorities Secretariat was at least prepared to admit that this model was deserving of serious scrutiny as a possible basis for reducing frictions between majority and minority nationalities.[38] In his examination, however, Krabbe claimed that the 1931 Nationalities Congress had failed to engage in real debate on the wider applicability of cultural autonomy beyond its Baltic heartland. What little discussion did take place had, according to Krabbe, focused uniquely on experiences in Estonia, a country where not all eligible minorities had actually seen fit to implement the 1925 cultural autonomy law. Outlining the various reservations that had already been voiced, not least in the context of the 1927 German–Polish crisis within the Congress, Krabbe concluded that Ammende and his colleagues had failed to make a convincing case as to why the League should recommend a more general application of cultural autonomy.[39]

Krabbe's analysis contains some pertinent reflections on the autonomy concept and the problems inherent in implementing this scheme. Interestingly, he suggested that alternative models of minority rights that were not based on the principle of formal enrolment and corporate organization might actually be more appropriate. Here he cited, among others, the system of autonomous minority schooling in Latvia, where a child's education was determined not on the basis of nationality, but rather according to the language most commonly spoken at home.

Ultimately, however, Krabbe's assessment betrays the enduring scepticism that League officials harboured towards what was still for most an entirely novel concept of collective minority rights. In Krabbe's words, a 'complete' solution to the minorities problem necessarily required:

> the development, in countries of mixed population, of a spirit of national tolerance and liberalism, a development which will be no less long and painful than that which took place in the sphere of religious tolerance, but which will become all the more difficult if a system of separatism in certain branches of the common life of the state becomes generalized.[40]

The unspoken assumption behind Krabbe's report was, therefore, that successful state- and nation-building in central and Eastern Europe would require, sooner rather than later, the assimilation of minorities into Western-style, one community nation states.

It is not without irony that Nationalities Congress activists had drawn the same parallel between religious and national tolerance, but had arrived at diametrically opposed conclusions. It was precisely the parallel between religious and cultural freedom that fuelled Paul Schiemann's vision of a Europe of multinational states, in which national ties across borders would be an essential component of enduring peace and greater unity. Symptomatically, Krabbe was deaf to the essential thrust of Schiemann's keynote speech at the 1931 Nationalities Congress, dismissing it as 'purely theoretical and philosophical'.[41] Yet in fact no message could have been more relevant to the times than this so-called philosophical analysis. In Schiemann's view the problems of Europe related to politicians basing their policies on 'fictions'. One such was that each state could balance its own economy, when in fact policies based on this assumption actually caused untold damage to neighbouring states. The second was that each European state could function as the bearer of a single national culture, which could be applied to all inhabitants. In reality, 'thousands, millions have their own culture and if these are forced to bow to alien beliefs then the state will be threatened; hatred will be born precluding peaceful coexistence within it'.[42]

It very much appeared as though the League of Nations and the Nationalities Congress – both claiming commitment to realizing and upholding minority rights – were in reality locked in a dialogue of the deaf. Two different visions of Europe's future underpinned their respective standpoints on minority rights. The one treated the issue largely in terms of protecting the integrity of the nation state and its borders by gradually assimilating minorities to the majority societal culture; the other conceived of the future Europe as a patchwork of national groups, wholly free like religious groups to maintain cultural ties with their co-nationals across geographical borders, thereby greatly reducing the practical significance of frontiers – a Europe of nations rather than indissolubly sovereign nation states.

For a brief period during the latter half of the 1920s, the Nationalities Congress vision of a Europe where territorial borders would in practice lose much of their significance could take some encouragement from a number of political schemes designed to reduce the risk of fresh conflict between European governments. These included the 1928 project for world peace launched by US secretary of state Frank Kellogg and French Foreign Minister Aristide Briand, who in the following year also elaborated his own proposals for European unity. Similar plans were outlined by other prominent pan-Europeanists, notably Richard Coudenhove-Kalergi and Karl Anton Prinz Rohan. Despite their conviction that state-led, top-down approaches could not in themselves achieve a lasting settlement of the national question, Nationalities Congress leaders recognized how the new debate on European unity might help to further their own cause of advancing minority rights.[43]

Optimism, however, proved to be all too short-lived. Instead of European governments adopting a common approach to the Great Depression of 1929, they reverted to more autarchic sovereign state solutions. Predictably, inter-ethnic disputes within states also sharpened as the economic situation worsened. By 1932 the Nationalities Congress was increasingly preoccupied by evidence of forcible assimilation in several European states, as exemplified by the 'decimation' of Slavic minorities in Italy and the violent 'pacification' of the Ukrainian minority in eastern Poland.[44] These disturbing trends were encapsulated in a speech entitled 'The new nationalist wave' (*Die neue nationalistische Welle*) that Paul Schiemann delivered to German minority leaders at Baden near Vienna on 26 June 1932.[45]

In an impassioned defence and reassertion of the original principles on which the Nationalities Congress had been founded, Schiemann drew a sharp distinction between what he called 'national sentiment' and 'nationalism'. In his exact words:

> Since nationalism at all times could be and was used to reinforce the citizen's feeling for the state, it was natural that the state showed itself concerned to nourish national sentiment and to anchor it in mass consciousness as the supreme civic virtue. Indeed, we in Europe today are universally prepared to acknowledge nationalism as a virtue enhancing humans and determining their inner being, without once asking what really is the essence of this virtue, the substance of this moral value. National sentiment is the feeling for the holiness of the ties forged by the national community. National sentiment is the recognition that only within the firm embrace of the culture of origin can humankind develop intellectually soundly and naturally. National sentiment is the individual's sense of responsibility for the fate of his people. National sentiment is a devoutness of mind. But, just as religious piety is a virtue only so long as it is a self-evident fundamental quality of the human spirit, manifesting itself in behaviour, but ceases to be a virtue once it is labelled as such and demands reward, so national sentiment also loses its moral worth once it ceases to count as the self-evident condition of human engagement in public life. That happens, however, the moment national sentiment is torn from the service of the community and made the basis of a party whose aim is the seizure of power within another community.[46]

In Schiemann's speech can be discerned a scarcely veiled attack on national socialism and its growing band of adherents amongst German minority groups across central and Eastern Europe. Symptomatically, Schiemann was addressing the organization that had originally called itself the *Verband der deutschen Minderheiten* [minorities] *in Europa*, but which by the end of the 1920s had been rebranded the *Verband der deutschen Volksgruppen* [ethnic groups] *in Europa*. Moreover, in another sign of the nationalist shift within the German minorities organization, Werner Hasselblatt assumed Carl-Georg Bruns' responsibilities in Berlin following the latter's death in 1931. The appointment was made in the face of strong objections from Paul Schiemann but, revealingly, with the full backing of Ewald Ammende.[47]

In the new nationalist wave speech, Schiemann lamented 'the unstoppable advance over all the peoples of Europe of the nationalist vision as a purported new ideology'.[48] This was the main reason, he contended, alongside the failure of League of Nations policy and the economic crisis, for the present dangerous situation of Europe. 'The feeling for national justice amongst the majority of people,' he continued, 'is deliberately undermined. The idea of fairness is made laughable as a doctrine, perceived as a weakness and as an unworthy sacrifice of nation state interests.'[49] Nothing exemplified this trend more dramatically than Hitler's subsequent assumption of power in Germany.

Most immediately, the Nazi policy of enforced dissimilation of Germany's Jews directly challenged what hitherto had been one of the key tenets of the Nationalities Congress – namely, the right of each individual freely to determine his/her own nationality. As a result of Hitler's actions, Leo Motzkin and other Jewish minority activists within the Nationalities Congress immediately launched an extensive campaign publicizing what was happening in Germany and trying to counter it. In the interests of impartiality, speakers at Congress meetings were not supposed to bring up specific grievances against individual state governments. In Motzkin's view, however, the unprecedented nature of Hitler's policy made a change in rules imperative if the Nationalities Congress was to retain any credibility as an organization defending minority rights.[50] He, therefore, insisted that leading representatives of the German minorities within the Congress join with other delegates in taking a clear and resolute stand against the deprivation of Jewish rights in Germany.[51]

While all German representatives were anxious for the Congress to continue, Motzkin's demand at once laid bare the deep divisions that had by now become manifest within the German minority movement. Paul Schiemann for his part tried to draft a resolution for the Congress condemning recent developments in Germany. His proposed declaration, however, failed to attract support from the majority of German representatives. A small group of German delegates to the *Verband* and the Congress, including the new *Verband* secretary Werner Hasselblatt, was already working to promote the national socialist agenda. Most of the remaining German delegates, including Ammende and recently appointed *Verband* president Hans Otto Roth from Romania, were reluctant to abandon entirely the founding principles of the Congress, but neither were they prepared to distance themselves from a resurgent Germany, not least because Berlin continued to provide the bulk of the funding for their organization.[52]

With the German group unwilling to issue any expression of solidarity with Jewish representatives about the persecutions in Germany, Nationalities Congress president Josip Wilfan sought desperately to paper over the cracks in an effort to keep the organization afloat. One suggestion Wilfan made was that German Jews should claim the status of national minority; in this way they could make use of existing international law with its at least nominal insistence upon equal rights and treatment for members of national minority groups. In effect, this would have entailed Jews long assimilated as Germans being forced to declare Jewish nationality. Any such suggestion, Motzkin countered, was 'degrading to humanity', rightly reminding Wilfan of his own words, spoken to stormy applause, the previous year: 'the right to assimilation, although we oppose this idea, we grant to anyone who wishes to assimilate: the obligation to assimilation we reject.'[53]

Wilfan's reasoning implied that Germany could legitimately reject Jewish claims to belong to a German *Volksgemeinschaft*, provided it did not deny Jews equal rights as citizens of Germany. This, of course, overlooks the fundamental fact that German Jews were being refused civil rights precisely on the basis of their ascribed ethnic, indeed purportedly racial, characteristics. Paul Schiemann for his part claimed that while one could not deny an ethnic group the right in certain circumstances to determine the boundaries of its own community,

> *Volkszugehörigkeit* [belonging to a people] rests not on a physiological but on a psychological state of affairs.... The

Volksgemeinschaft bears responsibility for all its members, tacitly or expressly a part of it, even when objective indicators point to membership of another nationality [*Volkstum*].[54]

Schiemann had intended to pronounce these words at the ninth meeting of the Nationalities Congress in Berne on 16–18 September 1933. However, since it was already clear before the Congress opened that his resolution would not be accepted by the German group, he opted not to attend the conference, citing grounds of recent illness.[55] Moreover, it was obvious by then that the Jewish delegates would also not be attending. Motzkin had written to Wilfan on 8 September from Geneva, where representatives of the Jewish minorities of Poland, Romania, Latvia (speaking also on behalf of Lithuania), Czechoslovakia and Bulgaria, present at the second World Jewish Congress, had agreed two resolutions. Since they had not received a satisfactory answer from the Nationalities Congress over the question of Jews in Germany, they resolved only to attend on the following conditions: first, that Wilfan, in agreement with the German group, put a resolution to the Congress expressly mentioning Germany and condemning its actions against Jews; second, that delegates be guaranteed in advance an unrestricted discussion of the German situation.[56]

Motzkin went out of his way to stress that these two conditions already represented a compromise, given that half of the Jewish representatives wanted to boycott the Nationalities Congress meeting outright. He demanded an answer by 13 September, failing which Jewish minority representatives would not attend. After subsequent exchanges by telegraph and letter between Wilfan and Motzkin, the governing council of the Nationalities Congress discussed the issue on the morning of 16 September. It unanimously decided that the point put by the Jewish groups on dissimilation and national rights, demanding an enlargement of the discussion and the formulation of a resolution which was critical of measures taken by a named state, could only take place by violating the established procedures of the Congress and, therefore, was not permissible.[57]

In his opening speech to the Congress, Wilfan was at great pains to emphasize the delicacy and complexity of decision-making in an organization where representatives had to demonstrate loyalty both to their own state and to their transborder national community. Symptomatically, his address made reference not to *German* policies, but to recent developments 'in a great European state'. Despite this, the Congress meeting was quite prepared to discuss the specific question of the Ukrainian famine and the actions of the Soviet government in this regard. Mikhail Kurchinskii gave a long speech on the issue, while Ukrainian delegate Milena Rudnicka declared her hope:

> that the congress will take the appropriate resolutions and address an appeal to the whole civilized world so that humanity's conscience does not have to be burdened with the dreadful complicity in the crime of the red Russian dictatorship in the Ukraine.[58]

The applause that greeted Rudnicka's remarks contrasted ominously with the refusal of delegates to sanction corresponding humanitarian initiatives in the case of Germany. This prompted one Jewish politician from Latvia to complain with justification that the sudden interest in nationality problems within the USSR was little more than a device to draw attention away from the growing influence of national socialism within the Nationalities Congress.[59]

Ammende, Roth and others had in fact already raised the Jewish question with the new regime in Berlin. In Ammende's case there was a meeting with Goebbels, although to judge from the latter's brief diary entry little progress was made. As to Roth, he managed to have a session with Hitler himself. The latter tried to give the impression that he had been forced to legislate and take action because of Jewish propaganda and defamation. In the course of his hour-long monologue he made it quite plain that everything was negotiable apart from the Jewish question. Declarations by Roth during the Congress on behalf of the German group duly followed the line that opposing assimilation necessarily precluded condemning dissimilation, even though this could 'sometimes be harsh'. Roth's specious reasoning conveniently glossed over the fact that the German government was removing basic civil and human rights, both through legislation and through force.[60]

The whole affair confirmed the impression that the Nationalities Congress had indeed thoroughly succumbed to the influence of the new German government. Any doubts on this score were removed by the wording of the resolution eventually adopted by delegates on the issue of national dissimilation and nationality rights. Echoing Wilfan's line, it cynically stated that, 'in the event of introducing national dissimilation the freedom and rights for which the Congress of European Nationalities has interceded in its procedures and resolutions since its founding remain inviolate'.[61] An additional declaration, put by Mikhail Kurchinskii on behalf of the remaining non-German minorities within the Congress, stated that 'the surge of expressly anti-Semitic measures currently to be seen in certain countries we regard as infringing general human rights and contradicting the ideals of our congress'. To this, Wilfan responded lamely that Kurchinskii had surely voiced the opinion of all members of the Congress, and wished to repeat his hope that Motzkin and other Jewish colleagues would continue their participation.[62]

Hardly surprisingly, Jewish representatives never again attended sessions of the Nationalities Congress. That was also true of Paul Schiemann, who for a while, alongside Josip Wilfan, held private talks with Jewish representatives in an attempt to keep Motzkin and his colleagues on board, the better to counter the obvious growth in Nazi influence.[63] This remained a vain hope. Ewald Ammende, who as general gecretary of the Congress had to be seen to be supportive of efforts at reconciliation, revealed his true inclinations in a private letter to Schiemann written from London on 10 June 1934. Casting doubt on the prospect for any agreement, Ammende went on to claim that: 'members of the German nation of Jewish religion who come here have only one wish – to assimilate as soon as possible in England: the majority does not think about preserving or fighting for its own nationality rights'.[64] It was also in this context that the *Verband der deutschen Volksgruppen* chose not to re-elect Schiemann to its board of management at its 1935 meeting in Gablenz where the Sudeten German national socialist Konrad Henlein assumed the leadership of the organization. At this point, Schiemann also wrote formally to Wilfan resigning his position in the Nationalities Congress.[65]

6 The new nationalist wave

Himself a victim of the new nationalist wave now sweeping Europe, Paul Schiemann had earlier predicted that in attacking the Jews, Hitler was forging the very weapon that would ultimately be used against the *Auslandsdeutschen*. The truth of this was soon to be confirmed by events in Schiemann's Baltic homeland, where the onset of economic depression had already created far more political space for those nationalist forces committed to undermining, even eliminating foreign influence and thereby building more 'complete' nation-states.[1]

In a *Rigasche Rundschau* editorial penned at the start of 1932, Schiemann had voiced his deep anxiety at the changes to Latvia's school system being proposed by Atis Ķēniņš, recently appointed minister of education.[2] Hitherto national minority education in Latvia had benefitted from the goodwill of the incumbent of this office. Previous ministers had on the whole allowed considerable latitude in interpreting the loose framework provisions of the 1919 law on minority schooling. Ķēniņš, however, now pointedly set about exploiting these very ambiguities in his pursuit of greater cultural homogeneity, or as local German leaders termed it, *Einheitskultur*.[3] The tactics employed by Ķēniņš included the use of special emergency decrees during parliamentary breaks.

Ķēniņš' strategy targeted, first and foremost, minority primary schools. By his own confession, the minister wished to turn all such schools into Latvian primary schools in which German, Russian and other minority languages served as mediums of instruction and nothing more. Without any consultation with the relevant minority sections within the ministry, Ķēniņš decreed that from 1 August 1932 all minority schools were to bring their curricula entirely into line with those of Latvian-language schools.

Moreover, instruction in minority primary schools was to be gradually transferred to teachers trained not in each nationality group's own institutions, but in the foreign language department of the Latvian Pedagogical Institute. Funding to develop this institution was to be diverted away from the corresponding minority training institutes under the 1932–1933 budget.[4]

A simultaneous decree stipulated that henceforth minority gymnasiums and professional schools could only be attended by pupils whose parents' 'national language' was that of the school in question. In the case of the Jewish minority, only Hebrew and Yiddish counted as national languages. Consequently, 25 Jewish schools teaching in German or Russian faced the prospect either of adapting their programmes or of closure.[5] A League of Nations report noted, however, that while Jewish schools were the most adversely affected by this ruling, the strongest and most vigorous protests against the new measures came from German minority representatives.[6]

Ironically, these changes were initiated under a coalition government headed by Marǵers Skujenieks, a man who had played an important role in advancing thinking on cultural autonomy among Latvians before and after the First World War and who in the 1920s had praised the Baltic Germans for their historic contribution to his country's well-being.[7] Ķēniņš, by contrast, now characterized Latvia as an 'Eldorado for minorities', in which Latvian peasants and workers were the objects of exploitation for the industry and trade of non-titular national groups.[8] Residual anxiety within the government about the possibly adverse impact of Ķēniņš' new course on external opinion eventually forced his Democratic Centre Party out of the ruling coalition, bringing about his own resignation. Nevertheless, the fact that his measures were not formally rescinded confirmed the extent of the continuing shift away from liberal minorities policy in the wake of the worldwide slump.

In neighbouring Estonia, state officials began even earlier to push their own more restrictive interpretation of the 1925 framework law on cultural autonomy. For example, it became apparent in the course of 1929 that what the German cultural council saw as its right to issue decrees for the management of German schooling could be frustrated by the minister of the interior. Although the minister was not empowered to annul such decrees he could, since cultural autonomy was exercised under his overall supervision, prevent their implementation on the grounds that they clashed with other state laws.[9]

Another pillar of Estonia's minority autonomy, namely the freedom to determine one's own ethnic affiliation, was also undermined by new legislation in 1928, prohibiting ethnic Estonians from adopting German nationality.[10] A further law in 1931 stipulated that henceforth only children holding German nationality would be entitled to enrol in German-language schools. Behind such measures lay obvious resentment at the allegedly privileged position enjoyed by German-language schools, which among other things had far smaller classes than their Estonian-language equivalents. It is little wonder that, under these conditions, ethnic Estonian parents continued to view German schooling as an attractive option for their children, particularly in the case of children from mixed marriages. The continued presence of Germanized Estonians (so-called *Kadakasakslased*) within an independent Estonia inevitably troubled more nationalistically minded political forces. State policies adopted during the late 1920s and early 1930s were clearly intended to limit the scope for cultural Germanization.

As Estonia's overall education budget came under increasing pressure at the start of the 1930s, the spotlight fell ever more on the anomalous position of German-language schools. In July 1931, education and social minister Jaan Piiskar announced universal cuts in secondary school provision. He envisaged an immediate reduction in the number of classes in the current year; by the end of the planned reform in 1934–1935 he expected only 895 secondary schools to remain, with an increase in the average number of pupils per class from 30 to 35. Staff reductions in the order of 70–75 posts were also anticipated.[11] The proposed cuts inevitably refocused attention on the budget allocation for German-language schools, which was calculated on the number of classes rather than on the numerical size of the German minority. Accordingly, it became easier for the government to justify a disproportionately high number of class closures in publicly funded German-language schools.[12]

By 1933, ministerial documents were also lamenting the large number of children from mixed Estonian–German marriages attending German-language schools. A report on an inspection of the Võru German-language public primary school claimed that of the 22 students enrolled, only 16 or 17 were German by nationality; of these, many were from mixed Estonian–German families, and thereby – it was implied – not genuinely native speakers of

German. This was significant because the law on primary schooling obliged the state to support a minority class only in areas where there were 20 pupils of the relevant nationality. In other words, restricting the right of educational choice in mixed families would at a stroke significantly reduce the number of German-language schools.[13]

The particularly close scrutiny of numbers in German-language schools was mirrored by closer ministerial oversight in the choice of textbooks for minority-language schools, especially notable when it came to the teaching of history. Correspondence during the summer of 1932 between the German cultural government and the ministry of education betrayed increasing vexation on the part of the latter. Officials expressed particular concern over a work by one A. Spreckelsen, school director and member of the German cultural council. Their complaint about his *Geschichte Estlands in Zusammenhang mit der Geschichte der Nachbarländer* was that it said too much about the neighbouring countries, thus making Estonia look a poor relation. While they were happy to note that the book did not go too deeply into the feats of the Teutonic Knights, they were less pleased to find not one single reference to General Johan Laidoner's leadership during Estonia's 1918–1920 war of liberation.[14] The list of books that had to be submitted for approval by the ministry continued to grow during the coming months.

The move away from liberal minority policy during 1931–1933 also reflected concern in Estonia and Latvia at a perceived growing external influence of national socialism on the Baltic Germans.[15] The implications of this for minority autonomy in Estonia can also be gleaned from the correspondence between the German cultural government and the ministry of education during the period. In one particular case the correspondence highlighted the concerns of the police commissioner in the town of Paide at the number of pupils from the local German school joining the newly formed Baltic–German Friends of the Scouts. The uniform of the organization, with its 'epaulettes and shoulder strap' was taken to be modelled on that of the Hitler Youth.[16] Similarly, the aforementioned county government report on the Võru German-language public primary school focused upon press articles alleging a growing influence of 'Hitlerism' amongst pupils. School director Fischmann felt impelled to formally deny that any of his pupils had worn the swastika. The German cultural government was also moved to deny further press reports that one pupil had entitled his essay on the anniversary of Võru's liberation from the Soviets, 'The March of Germans into Estonia', a claim that even the official report had to acknowledge was actually false.[17]

The concern shown by Baltic governments about the influence of national socialism amongst local ethnic Germans was understandably heightened once Hitler came to power in January 1933. Within two weeks of the event, the most prominent Baltic German critic of Nazism, Paul Schiemann, felt that he could no longer continue as editor of the *Rigasche Rundschau* in the face of growing interference from the German Foreign Office, which for the first time used the paper's financial dependence on it as a lever to influence its editorial line.[18] The new mood amongst far too many Latvian Germans was exemplified by an article in the *Baltische Monatshefte* by Erhard Kroeger, a key figure in the so-called *Bewegung* (movement) of the Baltic Germans. Under the heading 'Political Inversion', Kroeger ridiculed the liberal minority policy pursued by Schiemann and others as 'selling out': 'political inversion', he noted, 'is a woman who appears in many clothes. Her favourite costume is the rule of law.' Instead, Kroeger advocated struggle in political life and victory for the fittest.[19]

Figure 6.1 Drawing from Estonian ministry of education file comparing the uniform of Baltic German Scouts with that of the Hitler Youth.

In the case of Estonia, Nazi sympathizers had less purchase on the ethnic German population. Nevertheless, efforts by the *Bewegung* and its local leader Viktor von zur Mühlen to assume control of the *Deutsch-Baltische Partei in Estland* (DBP) during 1933 had severe consequences for the entire community. Following one failed bid at the DBP congress in April, von zur Mühlen was able to secure a majority on the party's ruling council and have himself elected leader in November. His bombastic assertion that 'a German and a national socialist are one and the same' did less than justice to the known dislike of the Nazis by such key Estonian German figures as Willhelm Von Wrangell, who now headed the German cultural council. Despite Wrangell's protestations that the cultural council was not synonymous with the DBP,[20] some Estonian politicians nevertheless insisted that the cultural council had become little more than a 'department of the German state within Estonia'.[21] The Estonian government was all too willing to exploit the occasion to remove von zur Mühlen. It also took the unprecedented step of suspending temporarily the activities of the German cultural council, although elections to the latter did ultimately go ahead as scheduled in March 1934.

In reality, a more immediate threat to governmental authority in both Estonia and Latvia came from home-grown nationalist extremism in the form of the Estonian League of Veterans of the War of Independence and the Pērkonkrusts. From the start of the 1920s, far-right extra-parliamentary movements had condemned the democracies of Estonia and Latvia as corrupt and weak, while calling for a more vigorously nationalizing line in all areas of state policy. These movements attracted more and more popular support at the start of the 1930s, when seemingly the established parties of the political centre were incapable of agreeing on effective measures to combat the economic depression.

Ultimately, the radical turn within these societies played into the hands of the conservative right, whose leaders Konstantin Päts and Kārlis Ulmanis had long advocated stronger, more centralized rule for the states they had been instrumental in founding after the First World War. With extremist movements on the point of gaining power in Estonia and making significant advances in Latvia, Päts and Ulmanis both ultimately seized the opportunity, respectively in March and May 1934, to suspend parliament and establish direct presidential rule.

A quick overview of the actions of Päts and Ulmanis thereafter belies the claim by both men that they had only 'seized power in defence of democracy'.[22] In the case of Päts, what was supposed to be a temporary six-month state of emergency evolved into a four-year 'era of silence'. This was followed by a constitutional reform in 1938 reintroducing token parliamentary institutions within what remained essentially a system of presidential, single-party rule. Ulmanis for his part never even bothered to initiate any comprehensive constitutional reform, but simply continued to rule by decree for the remainder of the decade.

The conservative peasant authoritarianism of Päts and Ulmanis consciously prioritized the interests of the titular nationality – embodied in their minds by the figure of the small private farmer – over those of national minorities.[23] While the minorities had never been especially well represented within the state bureaucracy, they were all but excluded after 1934. Similarly, the policy of concentrating more and more productive resources in the hands of the (national) state inevitably impacted disproportionately upon nationalities such as the Germans and the Jews. The relatively strong position that these had managed to preserve in key sectors of the economy during the 1920s was now seriously threatened.[24]

Measures adopted in Latvia at the start of 1935 placed new restrictions on the right of non-ethnic Latvians to practise as lawyers. Minorities were also effectively excluded from purchasing real estate, which from February 1935 required the permission of the justice minister. In the words of Ulmanis, the measure would prevent the formation of any further 'dead pockets' of Germans within Latvian society.[25] The Latvian Credit Bank established in April then made it much easier for the state to cut off the flow of finance to enterprises owned by non-ethnic Latvians; many of these were now compulsorily nationalized.[26] Finally, as part of the further corporate restructuring under the so-called Sylvester Laws of 31 December 1935, numerous private economic organizations were closed, and the historic buildings of the Little and Great Guilds confiscated by the state. The latter decision aroused unprecedented animosity within local German circles.

Ulmanis' reference to 'dead pockets' of Germans suggests a distinctly uncomfortable affinity with the sentiments expressed in the journal of the radical right *Pērkonkrusts* movement in October 1933. The journal trumpeted that:

[I]t is up to us Latvians how we act in our country. We shall decide your fate without you. You are a mere object in our hands. We will do what we think right. Using the same methods you used against us. Your time, you German people, is over ... In Latvia of the Latvians there is no room for you.[27]

To be fair, Ulmanis cannot reasonably be accused of sharing *Pērkonkrusts*' anti-Semitism, the public expression of which he prohibited. Latvia also remained one of the few countries in Europe that kept its doors open to Jewish refugees fleeing Nazi persecution during the 1930s. This, however, should not be taken as any kind of indication that Latvia's Jews enjoyed a privileged position under the new regime. Jews were by no means exempt from economic policies of nationalization, while politically Ulmanis essentially practised a strategy of divide and rule, maintaining his previously close relationship to Mordechai Dubin's *Agudat Israel*, the better to marginalize leftist and Zionist elements more ill disposed to the government.[28]

The political and economic changes from 1934 went hand-in-hand with a contraction of the cultural space previously afforded to minorities during the era of parliamentary democracy. In the crucial sphere of educational provision, the impact was immediate. On 12 July 1934, a mere two months after Ulmanis assumed absolute power, the 1919 law on minority schooling was abolished. Minority education now came under the terms of a general education law, which appeared on the statute book a week later.[29]

The new arrangements abolished the separate minority-school administrations within Latvia's ministry of education. In place of the former education chiefs with their experienced staff, there were now single advisors on minority education for each group. They were ill placed to cope with a workload that had almost overwhelmed the previous structures. In the case of the Jewish minority, *Agudat Israel*'s assumption of control over autonomous schooling prompted more secularly minded parents to remove their children from Hebrew and Yiddish schools and send them to establishments teaching in Latvian.[30] The new law also removed state and communal funding for separate minority pedagogical institutes and for institutions such as the German-run Riga Business School.

In what amounted to a far more serious blow to minority education in Latvia, the state was now only obliged to offer minority language education in those areas where there were 60 pupils speaking a particular language, as opposed to 30 under the former arrangements. Furthermore, pupils now had to be in the same catchment area, whereas previously it had been possible to organize a school for children drawn from neighbouring districts.[31] The overall effect of these measures was, of course, to bring about a further reduction in the number of minority-language schools by the middle of the 1930s. By 1935, for instance, the percentage of Russians receiving an education in their native tongue had declined from 90 to only 60 per cent.[32]

In Estonia, the German and Jewish cultural councils remained in existence, albeit within the framework of Päts' new non-democratic model of societal organization. In keeping with this, the institutions of autonomy were brought ever more firmly under the supervision of the ministry of education. As in Latvia, new legislation had the practical effect of reducing the numbers of those eligible to enrol in minority-language schools, most notably so by means of a decree of October 1934 stipulating that if one parent in a family was ethnically Estonian, the child had to attend an Estonian-language school.[33] The German cultural government had already protested that the proposed new policy disregarded the complexity of language use and national identity within ethnically mixed families. In its violation of the principles of individual choice contained in the 1920 Constitution, the latest step by the government was depicted as analogous to the Orthodox conversion campaigns conducted by the Tsarist Russian regime in the Baltic provinces during the 1840s.[34]

Inevitably, the new measures were seized upon with great relish by some local authorities within Estonia. A letter to the education ministry in March 1935 from a representative of the Kuresaare town council expressed distaste for previous 'ultraliberal' minority legislation that had allowed parents of Estonian origin to send their children to German-language schools at the expense of the state. It had not been easy, the missive remarked, for 'a nationally minded city council to allocate sums that are being used for the purpose of diverting children away from the nationality to which they rightly belong'.[35] Having examined public records, the council was pleased to discover that, according to the letter of the law, 20 out of 66 pupils attending the Kuresaare German-language public primary school were not entitled to be there. Other pupils at the school were found to belong to national minority groups that did not have cultural autonomy, and these too, it was urged, should have been enrolled in Estonian-language schools under the terms of the October 1934 decree.[36]

The school department of the German cultural government disputed this interpretation, claiming that the Kuresaare council was in fact obliged to continue funding education for 58 of the pupils currently at the school.[37] The German case was accepted by the ministry of education, suggesting that the cultural government was still able to find at least some measure of understanding on the part of central state institutions. As much is confirmed by accounts of regular conversations that Wilhelm von Wrangell and others had with President Päts.[38] Ultimately, however, the overall situation for Estonia's minorities continued to worsen as time wore on. A new language law adopted in October 1934 did not entirely exclude minority languages; they retained formal parity with Estonian within the courts. Yet their use was circumscribed not only within local authorities and public places, but also in the internal workings of the minority self-governments.[39] Another feature of these years was an official campaign for the Estonianization of surnames, a step undertaken by almost 80,000 of the country's inhabitants. Although the process was supposedly voluntary, minority officials complained that a failure to Estonianize one's name could have grave consequences for employment prospects.[40]

In a speech commemorating ten years of German cultural self-government in Estonia, Wilhelm von Wrangell underlined the importance of 'competent centralized representation' for minority interests, especially now at a time when ethnic communities faced a constant struggle against unfriendly decrees emanating from the state bureaucracy.[41] Wrangell's point applied to the German and Jewish minorities, but not to the Russian, whose leaders now began to regret the fact that they had not implemented cultural autonomy during the period of democratic rule. Having ignored Kurchinskii's warning at the start of the decade, Russian representatives belatedly redoubled their efforts to establish a national cultural corporation following the shift to authoritarian rule. Growing worries about enforced changes in state-controlled Russian schools, as well as increased official pressure to adopt Estonian family names, were potent factors. In the words of the Estonian daily *Vaba Maa*, the Pechory Russian 'hitherto knew only religious differences. Now he is learning about national differences and, therefore, begins to wish for cultural autonomy.'[42] Additional urgency was given by the fact that only organized minorities were to be allowed representation in the appointed upper chamber of Estonia's proposed new bicameral parliament, due to come into being on 1 January 1938.

In October 1937 a delegation from the Union of Russian Educational and Charitable Societies formally asked for permission to prepare for the introduction of Russian cultural autonomy. Mikhail Kurchinskii was to oversee the committee charged with establishing a national register and with organizing elections. It took only a few days for the government to reject the application on the grounds that a decision would have to await the introduction of new regulations for local self-government under the forthcoming new constitution. The promised new regulations for cultural authorities were in fact never passed.[43]

The constitutional order introduced in January 1938 came as a profound disappointment to all of Estonia's minorities, regardless of whether or not they had implemented cultural autonomy. The fundamental principle that all nationalities were equal before the law was retained. However, nationality was no longer deemed a matter of free choice for the individual, but was rather to be determined by law. Moreover, whereas the previous constitutions of 1920 and 1933 had enshrined the right to cultural autonomy, the new version spoke only of cultural self-*administration*. Also absent were guarantees of basic education in one's mother tongue: teaching in minority schools would be conducted both in the relevant minority language and in Estonian 'on the bases of and within the limits prescribed by law'. This lack of guarantees aroused particular concern within the German cultural government, where the feeling was that every new law seemed to be aimed at creating difficulties for national minorities.[44]

In terms of political representation, too, the new arrangements were less than ideal from a minority perspective. The lower house of parliament was popularly elected, but according to a first-past-the-post principle rather than under the previous system of proportional representation, which had benefited dispersed groups such as the Germans. A request from the German cultural government for special dispensation in the form of an extraterritorial constituency was not granted.[45] Moreover, the 1938 Constitution stipulated that henceforth representation of minorities would be entrusted to just a single deputy within the upper chamber of parliament. In 1938–1939 this task fell to Dr Helmuth Weiss, who acted as the representative of the German and Jewish minorities.

Weiss' role confirms that the control exerted by the Nazis over the German community in Estonia was less pronounced than it was in neighbouring Latvia.[46] Here the Baltic German *Volksgemeinschaft* fell increasingly under the influence of Erhard Kroeger and his supporters, following Paul Schiemann's departure for Vienna in 1933 and the dissolution of Latvia's political parties. Despite the differences between Latvia and Estonia, ethnic Germans in both countries were by this time increasingly looking towards the Reich as their protector. In that respect the points were being set that would lead eventually to the wholesale resettlement of the Baltic German population to Polish lands conquered by Nazi Germany and cleared of their rightful inhabitants following the start of the Second World War.

Similarly, as war again loomed over the lands between Germany and the Soviet Union, many ethnic Russians living in Latvia and Estonia were becoming increasingly disenchanted with their situation. Their mood was beginning to feed a growth in pro-Soviet sentiments among sections of the Russian community, notably the leftist intelligentsia as well as the peasantry in the eastern districts of Estonia. Already at the start of 1939, Russian members of the Estonian parliament and the leaders of the Union of Russian Educational and Charitable Societies had signed an appeal to President Päts protesting at the poor economic situation of the Russian peasantry, as well as at the lack of opportunity for social advancement and employment within the state apparatus. They also complained of growing efforts to forcibly Estonianize the Russian minority, especially those living in the borderlands.[47]

The appeal claimed that Estonia's network of Russian-language schools was being destroyed, citing the fact that around a third of such institutions in the Pechory and Prichuda districts were now headed by Estonians, some of whom could barely speak Russian. One example concerned a Russian primary school, again in Pechory town, where out of seven teachers most were not properly qualified and only one was Russian. To make matters worse, there had been a steady reduction in the number of subjects taught in the Russian language. Even ethnic Russian conscripts for the military, it was alleged, were being forced to endure verbal attacks against their people and culture.[48]

Claims of growing tensions were echoed by state officials, many of whom were only too happy to witness the mass departure of Baltic Germans from Estonia from mid-October 1939 onwards.[49] Similar jubilation was expressed by official circles in Latvia, where the first resettlement ship sailed from Riga on 7 November 1939. Latvia's interior minister said of those people hitherto counted as German who had not taken up the option of German citizenship but chosen to remain in their homes at the cut off date of 15 December: '[T]hey were German neither by inclination nor blood, for then they would not have remained here.' After 15 December, he insisted, there would be neither a German national group nor Germans in Latvia. Those who decided not to leave 'can no longer call themselves Germans'.[50] The pro-Ulmanis newspaper *Brīvā Zeme* commented that: 'Not everything is accomplished with the departure of the Germans. Let this event move us at the same time to free our country and people from the traces of German culture.'[51]

Despite the triumphalist tone of official propaganda, many Latvians and Estonians were only too aware that the so-called *Umsiedlung* (resettlement) of Baltic Germans portended the end of the independent states established two decades earlier. Back in 1920, Paul Schiemann had warned that it would not be difficult to destroy Latvia's German minority. He added, however, that 'at the very moment when the last German ceases to feel himself a Latvian citizen, when we have mentally to withdraw from the society of our home, Latvia's fate must and will be decided'.[52] Two decades later, Schiemann justified his own personal decision to reject the *Umsiedlung* and remain in the country where he had struggled for so long to promote the coexistence of different ethnicities within a shared territorial space. In his view, this remained the only viable option for the future of Europe. The *Umsiedlung* itself, he argued, confirmed that the alternative of homogenizing political space necessarily rested on force, in that some individuals would always resist leaving through love of homeland. Ultimately then, resettlement would mean that 'all the unspeakable human suffering that the Jewish laws have caused [in Germany] must be increased tenfold throughout Europe'.[53]

As ever, the prescience of Schiemann's words is striking. By the time he penned these lines, at some point in the spring of 1940, his homeland of Latvia was about to experience the apogee of what has been termed Europe's 'age of extremes'.[54] The Soviet occupation in June of that year quickly exposed the country's inhabitants to brutal Stalinist policies of social cleansing. The deportations and killings of 1940–1941 then gave way to the genocide against the Jews perpetrated by German forces and local collaborators following the Nazi invasion of the Baltic area in summer 1941.[55] Paul Schiemann experienced both wartime occupying regimes, albeit from the vantage point of his home in a Riga suburb, to which he was by now confined both by debilitating illness and – from 1941 – by a state of house arrest imposed by the Nazi authorities.[56]

The events unfolding around Schiemann could hardly have come as a greater blow to the ideals he had campaigned for within the European nationalities movement. This was doubtless made all the more painful by the knowledge that some of his Baltic German former co-workers were by now actively colluding in Hitler's plans to displace non-German populations from occupied Soviet territory in his quest to attain *Lebensraum* for the German *Volk*. In particular, Schiemann's earlier misgivings regarding Werner Hasselblatt were amply confirmed. This former architect of German cultural autonomy in democratic Estonia was at this stage to be found writing memoranda for Alfred Rosenberg's Reich Ministry for the Occupied Eastern Territories.[57]

Paul Schiemann and his wife nevertheless remained wholly true to their ideals by sheltering a young Jewish woman from Riga, Valentina Freimane, following the murder of her family by the Nazis. Freimane remained with the Schiemanns until Paul's death under Nazi occupation in June 1944. She survived the war and continued to live in Latvia. She currently divides her time between Riga and Berlin, and remains the last living witness to Schiemann's final days. Her testimony confirms his enduring conviction that his vision of a democratic and multicultural Europe would in time prevail, despite the horrors then being visited upon the continent.[58]

7 Cultural autonomy
A new chapter?

The Second World War is synonymous, particularly in Eastern Europe, with genocide, ethnic cleansing and displacement of peoples. Forced population movements in the region did not cease in 1945, but were endorsed in the immediate post-war period, even by the Western democracies, as a solution to the nationality conflicts that had proved so intractable between 1919 and 1939. In the aftermath of the war, the Western victor powers subsumed the concept of minority rights within that of individual human rights, as promulgated most notably by the United Nations. In 1953, the recently established Council of Europe endorsed the European Convention for the Protection of Human Rights and Fundamental Freedoms. In affirming that the liberties secured by the Convention were applicable to all, this document made no specific provisions for belonging to a national minority, beyond the obvious safeguards against differential treatment on the grounds of ethnicity.[1]

Subsequently, within the context of the geopolitical stability imposed by the Cold War, it was assumed on both sides of the Iron Curtain that ethnicity would ultimately cease to be a significant factor in public life. Ethnic diversity in varying degrees remained a feature of all European states, both East and West, but the dominant expectation in the immediate post-war decades was that such differences were likely to lose any meaning under the inexorable onward march of modernization.[2] As had been the case after the First World War, the implication was that all minority ethnicities would ultimately be merged into homogenous nation states.

The subsequent reality proved to be rather different. Writing in 2007, Will Kymlicka observed that:

In the last 40 years, we have witnessed a veritable revolution around the world in the relations between states and ethno-cultural minorities. Older models of assimilationist and homogenizing nation states are increasingly being contested, and often displaced, by newer 'multicultural' models of the state and citizenship. This is reflected, for example, in the widespread adoption of cultural and religious accommodation for immigrant groups, the acceptance of territorial autonomy and language rights for national minorities, and the recognition of land claims and self-government rights for indigenous peoples.[3]

This multicultural turn was in the first instance a response to growing immigration to Western Europe from the 1960s onwards, as well as to the development or revival of ethno-regionalist movements in states such as Belgium and Spain. The process was accelerated by the largely unanticipated political changes occurring in Eastern Europe during the second half of the 1980s.

Here, developments within the USSR above all increasingly cast doubt upon official proclamations by the Soviet regime that the nationality question had been solved and distinct ethno-national identities definitively subsumed within a new overarching concept of 'Soviet people'. In reality, in the context of territorially institutionalized multi-ethnicity and undemocratic, centralized rule by Moscow, many residents of the non-Russian republics came to view what was termed sovietization as synonymous with russification.[4] Growing emphasis on the public use of the Russian language across all the Soviet republics, together with ongoing migration of Russian-speakers to the borderlands, heightened fears that the federal structure of the USSR, with its long-standing cultural supports for non-Russian nationalities, was set to disappear. The prospect contributed to a visible rise in social tensions in some regions by the 1980s, including the Baltic republics of Estonia and Latvia, where sustained post-war immigration had increased the Russian-speaking share of the population to 39 and 48 per cent respectively.

When Mikhail Gorbachev's policies of *glasnost* (openness) and democratization loosened political controls in the mid-1980s, new nationalist movements quickly developed across the USSR, greatly hastened by the failure to reverse an ongoing decline of the Soviet economy. Nationalist movements were at their most effective in the Baltic republics of Estonia, Latvia and Lithuania, where it was possible to mobilize hundreds of thousands of local residents behind a peaceful campaign in support of full independence. What became known as the 'singing revolution' drew upon the collective memory of interwar statehood and its violent suppression, as well as – in the case of the Estonian and Latvian movements – notions of an existential threat to the language and societal culture of the republics' titular nationalities.

While support for ethno-regionalism was at its most pronounced in the Baltic area, the Soviet central government soon had to contend with a parade of sovereignties by all republics, including, from May 1990, the Russian Republic.[5] As had previously been the case with the collapse of the Tsarist Russian Empire, however, the subsequent demise of the USSR in 1991 did not solve the nationality question, but merely recast it in a different form.[6] The legacy of territorially institutionalized multi-ethnicity ensured that tensions quickly emerged between new nationalizing states, national minorities and external national homelands. Here a particular focus of attention has been the estimated 25 million ethnic Russians currently residing outside the borders of the Russian Federation, itself home to 120 different ethnic groups.

Similar dynamics manifested themselves within the Yugoslav Federation at the turn of the 1990s, albeit with far more destructive consequences. In central Europe, post-1989 processes of political and social transformation occurred within what were ostensibly more secure state borders. Yet here too, nationality issues soon manifested themselves, as witnessed by the Czech–Slovak so-called velvet divorce of 1993 and the renewed discussions surrounding the status of the sizeable ethnic Hungarian minorities living in Slovakia, Romania, Serbia and Ukraine, as well as their relationship both to their states of residence and to their putative external national homeland of Hungary.[7]

In a rather sudden and dramatic fashion, therefore, the eastern part of Europe was again confronted with the dilemma of how to accommodate political movements seeking cultural recognition for particular ethnic groups without '[undermining] the already fragile civic cohesion of multiethnic countries and [reinforcing] a parochial approach to politics amongst their constituent nationalities'.[8] The demise of the USSR, and of Yugoslavia in particular, gave impetus to renewed discussions on a European minority-rights regime that had finally begun in 1990 under the auspices of the Conference (later Organization) for Security and Co-operation in Europe (henceforth OSCE).[9] In what appeared to be a far reaching provision, the OSCE in 1992 created the post of High Commissioner for National Minorities (HCNM), with the power to make pronouncements and recommendations on the protection of minorities within particular OSCE member states, regardless of the relevant government's wishes in the matter. Individual governments could also compel any other member state to admit fact-finding delegations and the establishment of longer term missions to assess and regulate ethnic relations.

The vision informing this work at the outset was for a truly universal minority-rights regime embracing all sovereign states in the zone stretching east from Vancouver to Vladivostok. The practice, however, recalled the shortcomings of the League of Nations in the aftermath of the First World War. Western governments, notably those of Britain, France, Spain, Turkey and indeed the United States, were not only unwilling to countenance any dilution of their sovereign rights, but in some cases even refused to acknowledge the existence of national minorities within their own borders, despite sometimes obvious evidence to the contrary. In keeping with this the attentions of the OSCE High Commissioner have focused firmly on the countries of Eastern Europe. These have also had to demonstrate 'respect for and protection of minorities' as one of the preconditions for entering the Council of Europe and, most significantly of all, the European Union – a state of affairs placing Western governments in a strong position to dictate conditions to former communist states seeking EU membership.

The heightened attention given to Eastern Europe has often been justified by reference to the ethnic violence that broke out in the former Yugoslavia and USSR during the early 1990s. Those events also revived interest in the concept of non-territorial cultural autonomy as a possible model for managing ethnic diversity in the region.[10] From the point of view of international organizations and national governments alike, cultural autonomy has been considered as a means of forestalling demands from national minorities for the kind of territorial autonomy that previously existed within Yugoslavia and the USSR, and which – more substantively – has been introduced in a number of Western European states over the past half-century.[11] From the point of view of national minority representatives, territorially based devolution may be seen as a logical facet of post-communist democratization. Yet central governments and indeed external agencies have tended rather to view it as potentially detrimental to state integrity. In that respect, cultural autonomy has been held up as a less destabilizing approach to addressing minority rights claims across central and Eastern Europe.

Indeed, the constitutional accommodation of ethnic diversity within existing borders has been a key preoccupation of the European Commission for Democracy through Law, better known as the Venice Commission. Established in 1990, it has served as an advisory body to the Council of Europe, which in 1995 adopted its own Framework Convention for the Protection of National Minorities (henceforth FCNM). In May 2007 the present authors helped to organize one of the Venice Commission's regular joint academic–practitioner Universities for Democracy seminars in Zagreb, Croatia, where they briefed participants on the historic experience of cultural autonomy in the region.[12]

The Venice Commission's interest in our work was stimulated by an earlier briefing that we were invited to give to government ministers in Romania at the start of 2005, when the country's parliament was drafting a new law on national minorities, ahead of accession to the EU. The event was arranged at the behest of the ethnic Hungarian party within Romania's then ruling coalition, the Democratic Union of Hungarians in Romania (in Hungarian, UDMR). UDMR's rationale for advocating non-territorial cultural autonomy as the basis for the legislation was to counter Romanian nationalist claims that minority autonomy would open the way to separatist demands on the part of the Hungarian minority, specifically a revival of Hungarian claims to sovereignty over the historically disputed territory of Transylvania.[13]

Similar concerns for preserving the territorial integrity of the state lay behind the Russian Federation's law on national-cultural autonomy, adopted in 1996. Its original purpose was to undercut the inherited Soviet model of ethno-territorial federalism as part of an effort to instil a more cohesive concept of Russian (*Rossiiskii*) political community founded on the post-1992 boundaries of the Russian Federation.[14] For Valerii Tishkov, chair of Russia's State Commission on Nationalities during the immediate post-Soviet era, a non-territorial model of ethnic rights was considered helpful in strengthening a popular sense of belonging to a single, multi-ethnic state community. The introduction of such a system appeared all the more logical given that in the case of many of the country's larger non-Russian nationalities, a considerable proportion of the group in question actually resided outside the borders of its designated territorial homeland; many smaller groups had previously enjoyed no recognition at all.[15]

If institutional density is taken as a measure, the Russian law of 1996 can be counted as a success, with over 250 bodies of national cultural autonomy established across the Russian Federation during the period 1996–2000.[16] Initial characterizations of the new law as 'Austro-Marxism's last laugh', however, proved premature, in so far as the powers and resources allocated to these new bodies were extremely limited. Indeed, in practical terms there was little to differentiate them from existing non-governmental organizations.[17] Under Tishkov's original proposals developed in 1992, the institutions of cultural autonomy were to have had a legal standing equal to that of the national republics within the federation. What emerged in reality was a much-attenuated version of these proposals, whereby national cultural autonomy functioned as a supplement to an essentially unchanged system of territorial autonomy. In recent times, moreover, national autonomy in whatever form has come under growing pressure due to the more centralizing and nationalizing impulses increasingly evident since the start of Vladimir Putin's presidency in 2000.

In Estonia, where the celebrated interwar law on cultural autonomy was revived to great fanfare in 1993, prospects for a successful practical application of the legislation have also been undermined by the nationalizing practices of the state. Post-independence, no automatic right to citizenship was extended to the large Russian-speaking speaking population of Soviet-era settlers and their descendents who made up 30 per cent of Estonia's total inhabitants in 1991. In the eyes of the restored Estonian Republic, these settlers do not constitute a genuine national minority, even though many have since obtained Estonian citizenship through naturalization. It would, therefore, appear that the reinstatement of the interwar cultural autonomy law was primarily a symbolic gesture. Its main aim was to counter international criticism of citizenship and other legislation and thus enhance Estonia's reputation in the eyes of its new Western partners, thereby improving the country's prospects for integration into international structures.[18]

Thus far the Estonian law has been implemented only by representatives of the country's Ingrian Finnish and Swedish minorities. Both groups are numerically small and territorially dispersed. Indeed, Estonia's Swedish-speaking minority was moved wholesale to Sweden in 1943, and most descendents of this group continue to live there.[19] Members of other numerically small minority nationalities in Estonia, such as the Belorussian community, have actively discussed the possibility of cultural autonomy. Yet most non-titular nationalities living in Estonia remain subdivided into citizens and non-citizens. For this reason, smaller groups have typically resorted to a law on non-commercial organizations as a basis for developing their own cultural societies and schools, rather than opting for full cultural autonomy.[20]

At 25 per cent of the population, ethnic Russians constitute by far and away the largest minority within today's Estonia. In the Soviet period, Russians, as the 'first amongst equals' of the Soviet nationalities had uniquely enjoyed access to extraterritorial cultural autonomy in the sphere of education and language use. The Soviet system thus bequeathed a network of Russian-language primary and secondary schools alongside those teaching in Estonian. While moves are currently afoot to shift to bilingual education at the upper secondary level, Russian-language schools have continued to operate under local authority auspices since 1991. Aside from the citizenship issue alluded to above, a reluctance to put at risk what is already in place is a major factor behind the reluctance of Russian-minority leaders to take up the option of cultural autonomy. As was the case between the wars, there are also concerns about the prospect of paying additional taxation for Russian schooling.[21]

The state of political marginalization occasioned by the citizenship law means that cultural autonomy would not in itself resolve current issues between the Estonian state and its Russian minorities. Despite renewed consideration of this option, for example in connection with current changes to state-funded Russian-language schooling, the tone amongst many Russian political leaders remains one of scepticism.[22] As was the case with the Baltic Germans between the wars, the Russian-speaking political elite in today's Estonia divides into those who are ready to embrace national minority status within a unitary state, and those who argue for a return to the bilingual, binational model of statehood of the Soviet-era. The latter suggestion is anathema as far as the majority of ethnic Estonian politicians is concerned; however, even more conciliatory Russian advocates of the minority rights model have struggled to make their voices heard, within a post-colonialist nation-building project as yet preoccupied with reversing perceived historical injustices perpetrated against the titular nationality during the period of Soviet rule.

Historically conditioned distrust between ethnic majority and minority also proved hard to overcome in the case of Romania, where the cultural autonomy law presented to parliament in 2005 eventually foundered. In yet another echo of the interwar period, it has to date proved impossible to settle disputes over the degree of powers to be allocated to the proposed minority cultural self-governments and over the question of who is to appoint them – the government or the minorities themselves. As an organic law, the draft bill of 2005 required the assent of both houses of the Romanian parliament and with only a slim overall majority the government was unable to command this.[23]

Non-territorial cultural autonomy has proved rather less controversial in neighbouring Hungary. In 1993 it became the first state to adopt a law on this basis following the fall of communism. A remarkable 96 per cent of Hungary's parliamentarians voted in favour of legislation that was adopted primarily with an eye to championing the rights of ethnic Hungarians living in neighbouring states.[24] From the standpoint of the government in Budapest, cultural autonomy could hardly be construed as threatening to the integrity of the Hungarian state. The overall proportion of national minorities within Hungary's population is numerically small and many of these are well integrated with the majority culture. Moreover, the territorially dispersed nature of minority settlement in Hungary has lent itself to a non-territorial model of autonomy.[25]

Once again, the existing literature has focused as often as not on the deficiencies of Hungary's 1993 law. Authors have noted that due to memories of past persecution members of minorities, such as the Roma and the Germans, were reluctant to declare publicly their ethnicity by enrolling on a national register. Thus, under the initial law of 1993, elections to minority self-governments were not conducted on the basis of national registers but were instead open to all citizens residing in a particular electoral district, regardless of ethnicity. Not surprisingly, this has in a number of cases led to problems of representativeness and legitimacy of the elected minority bodies, including the phenomenon of so-called ethno-business, whereby political entrepreneurs have been able to pose as minority representatives simply in order to gain access to public office and the entitlements that flow from this.

As a result of such anomalies, Hungary's cultural autonomy law was eventually amended in 2005 and an obligatory system of enrolment on national registers – for candidates and voters alike – was introduced.[26] Some critics, however, remain implacably opposed to the concept of minority cultural autonomy per se, regardless of how the bodies are elected. As regards the Roma minority in particular, it is argued by some that granting autonomy is a lot easier and indeed less costly than getting to grips with the most pressing problem facing this community, namely deep-seated discrimination and socio-economic marginalization at the hands of the state and the Magyar majority. Without parallel action to deal with this issue, it is said, cultural autonomy runs the risk of exacerbating the exclusion of the Roma, by entrenching pre-existing ethnicized boundaries within society. In some cases Hungarian local authorities have stood accused of abrogating their social and economic responsibilities to Roma constituents, on the specious grounds that these now fall within the remit of minority self-government.[27]

Despite all such problems, cultural autonomy has almost certainly helped to boost both the cultural self-awareness of Hungary's minorities and their participation in public life, all the more so given that autonomous bodies have possessed rights of advocacy in relation to the state authorities. More than 1,200 minority self-governments have come into existence across Hungary since the mid-1990s, and it is notable that over half of these have been established by representatives of the Roma, the country's largest minority group. To speak approvingly of cultural autonomy is not to deny the very real problems of discrimination and social exclusion still faced by the Roma minority; however, the fact that growing numbers of people have apparently been willing to identify themselves as Roma in state census returns would seem to suggest that their situation is more favourable than in some neighbouring countries of the region.[28]

More generally, recent discussions of cultural autonomy within central and Eastern Europe have dovetailed with contemporary debates on European integration and the future of the nation state. Here too, the discussions conducted within the 1920s Nationalities Congress often appear startlingly relevant. According to some recent accounts, for instance, there is a possibility that Europe's Roma might be granted the status of a transnational minority with its own targeted rights regime within the European Union, thus resurrecting an idea propagated by Jewish representatives from central and Eastern Europe in the immediate aftermath of the First World War.[29]

Yet, as the case of Hungarians in Romania illustrates very clearly, there remains a high degree of political sensitivity regarding any suggestion of enhanced cross-border links between minorities and their external national homelands. The continued climate of mistrust in this regard was especially apparent during the discussions surrounding Hungary's 2001 so-called status law, whereby the government in Budapest sought to extend certain entitlements to ethnic Hungarians living in neighbouring countries. Once more echoing the Nationalities Congress debates of the 1920s, the Hungarian prime minister and initiator of the legislation, Viktor Orban, also expounded his vision of how a future 'Europe of national communities' might evolve within the overall context of a deepening and widening European Union.[30]

Orban's initial proposal met with a distinctly wary response from the European Union and other relevant international bodies, such as the Council of Europe's Venice Commission and the OSCE. All denounced Hungary's pretensions as an external homeland to its co-nationals abroad. The main objection related to talk of a trans-sovereign Hungarian nation and to the inclusion within the law of social welfare as well as cultural entitlements. In this respect, international organizations insisted that persons belonging to minorities have to be seen first and foremost as citizens of their state of residence, and that this state must bear the primary responsibility for their welfare. Furthermore, it was established that the proposed status law violated the principle of equality by discriminating on the basis of ethnic origin between citizens of foreign states.[31] This finding seemingly underlined the continued primacy of the nation state concept within the European Union and the international system more widely.

For all this, the idea of a Europe of nationalities still merits closer scrutiny. The international deliberations on Hungary's status law may have refuted the concept of a trans-sovereign nation, but in doing so they did not entirely discount the notion that national governments can legitimately maintain ties with ethnic kin minorities living beyond their borders.[32] Under the terms of the Council of Europe's Framework Convention on National Minorities, Hungary is entitled, subject to bilateral treaties with neighbouring states, to promote Hungarian language and culture abroad. In as much as cultural and linguistic ties were at the heart of the efforts by the Nationalities Congress to unite ethnic communities across state borders, the relevant provisions of the FCNM do not appear too far removed from the ideas floated back in the late 1920s.

More broadly, the EU, Council of Europe and OSCE are all today committed to working within existing state borders to create a new multicultural understanding of shared territorial space within central and Eastern Europe. This is an approach with which the leaders of the 1920s minorities movement would wholeheartedly concur. After all, the primary concern of Paul Schiemann and others was not with state borders as such, but with persuading each individual to work for the good of the *place that he or she inhabits*. In this regard, the Congress programme represented an effort to adapt Renner and Bauer's original model – coined in an age of multinational empires – to the new realities of the modern nation state system.

Today, it is perhaps even more fanciful to posit (as Renner and Bauer surely did a century ago) that the conceptual link between ethnicity and territory can be broken entirely. Territorially based devolution for minorities has become commonplace within the longer established democracies of the Western world during the last half a century. Therefore, it seems unlikely that larger and more territorially concentrated minorities living in central and Eastern Europe will be willing to eschew this model in favour of a purely non-territorial form of autonomy. Despite this, Karl Renner's central contention – that territorial approaches alone cannot definitively regulate the nationality question – remains as valid today as ever. Ethnic and political boundaries in Europe will never be completely congruent and some members of national minorities will inevitably fall outside a territory 'of their own'. In this respect, non-territorial cultural autonomy retains at the very least the potential to complement other, territorially based models of minority rights.

Minority rights remain a contentious, securitized issue within the societies of central and Eastern Europe, where latent conflicts between states, national minorities and external national home-lands continue to exist both across the external EU frontier (in the case, for example, of Russian minorities in the Baltic states) as well as within the European Union itself (in the case of Hungarian minorities in Slovakia and Romania). The central and East European situation and accompanying debates on cultural autonomy in the region must also be viewed within the context of broader European and global contemporary discussions of multiculturalism and societal cohesion. As Europe's East and West converge within common institutional frameworks, interesting questions arise not simply about the capacity of the EU and other bodies to advance post-communist democratization, but also about the potential relevance of home-grown East European models of multiculturalism for Western Europe and, indeed, beyond.

There are in fact already a number of examples outside central and Eastern Europe where the principles of non-territorial cultural autonomy have been applied during recent decades. One obvious instance relates to indigenous peoples such as the Maori in New Zealand and the Saami in the Nordic countries. Beyond this, non-territorial autonomy has been a facet of consociational political systems of government in multinational states, perhaps most notably the Belgian model operating since the 1970s. Of this it has been said that 'the plan to devolve power simultaneously to three regions (Flanders, Wallonia and Brussels) and to two communities (the Dutch- and French-speaking ones) is a close replica of Renner's original scheme for the Austrian Empire'.[33] Even if – as some now suggest – Flanders and Wallonia were to go their separate ways in the near future, the system of communal cultural autonomy would surely have to remain as part of the overall settlement. One could also envisage further instances where cultural autonomy might in future come into play, for example as part of a longer term settlement of the Irish question.

Opinion remains more divided over whether the cultural autonomy model (or aspects thereof) might have applicability to the systems of immigrant multiculturalism developed in post-war Western Europe and north America.[34] In this respect, it is perhaps worth noting that the original model of Renner and Bauer was inspired to a large extent by the vision of itinerant workers taking their culture with them wherever they moved (albeit within the shared territorial and political frame of the Habsburg state). Yet subsequent academic and political discussions of minority rights (including those during the 1920s) have customarily drawn a distinction between historically rooted *national* minorities and indigenous peoples on the one hand and 'immigrant', 'ethnic' or 'new' minorities on the other. Substantial national-cultural autonomy of the kind envisaged by Renner and Bauer is generally deemed to be the preserve of the former, whereas the latter typically seek (and by implication are supposed to be content with) a more modest level of recognition of their distinct identity.[35]

Traces of past reflections on national-cultural autonomy can, however, be discerned in recent and ongoing discussions in the United Kingdom around what has been termed faith-based multiculturalism. The past decade and a half in particular has seen a number of policy initiatives, drawing on communitarian thinking, that seek to bring together religion, community and social cohesion.[36] Against this background, former British Labour Party member of parliament and onetime home secretary Charles Clarke made a speech to the Royal Commonwealth Society in November 2006 in which he argued that 'the left ought to be more sympathetic to at least the practice of faith'. Clarke went on to describe faith as 'generally a force for good', whose 'general practice is to respect other faiths and foster good relations and tolerance between them'. In this respect, he continued:

> I believe that the state ought to encourage a stronger formal relationship with the main faith communities. For example we should make it unequivocally clear that it is perfectly appropriate for faith-led voluntary and community organizations to receive support from public funds on the same basis as those which are not faith-led.[37]

More controversially, in February 2008 the Archbishop of Canterbury, Rowan Williams, delivered a lecture entitled Civil and Religious Law in England: a Religious Perspective. By his own account, Williams was seeking 'carefully to explore the limits of a unitary and secular legal system in the presence of an increasingly plural (including religiously plural) society and to see how such a unitary system might be able to accommodate religious claims'.[38] Citing existing Orthodox Jewish practice in relation to the jurisdiction of British courts, he suggested that under certain circumstances Sharia law might also serve as an 'overlapping jurisdiction' under which individuals might choose to seek justice. This was on the understanding that 'no supplementary jurisdiction could have the power to deny access to the rights granted to other citizens or to punish its members for claiming those rights'.[39]

The relevance of Williams' proposals to the original ideas of Renner and Bauer (and the debates of the 1920s) is, of course, open to question, both in relation to the faith-based aspects and the advocacy of multiple legal systems.[40] There is, nevertheless, an interesting point of comparison to be found in the Archbishop's opening contention that if the law fails to engage adequately with particular communities, this can '[open] up real issues of power by the majority over the minority, with potentially harmful effects for community cohesion'.[41] This basic point was, however, lost in the media storm elicited by Williams' lecture.[42]

The Williams furore indicated the extent to which public discussion of such themes in the UK has been adversely affected by the 'multiculturalism backlash' evident in Western societies since the mid-1990s.[43] Directed first and foremost at immigrant multiculturalism – and at Islamic minorities in particular – this reaction has been largely driven by right-wing political groups amongst the majority population who assert that state multiculturalist policies have gone too far and have begun to threaten what is termed the majority way of life. Securitization of the issue and 'othering' of Islamic communities have been given additional momentum by the 11 September 2001 attacks in New York and the subsequent wars in Afghanistan and Iraq. At the same time, elements of the centre-left in Western democracies have also begun to question the pre-existing course of immigrant multiculturalism, arguing that there has been a failure to properly address the sources of minorities' social, economic and political exclusion. Indeed, it is claimed that these policies may inadvertently have contributed to greater communal segregation and isolation.[44]

The core idioms of the multiculturalism backlash include the notion that multicultural state policies foster separateness, reject common values, support 'culturally reprehensible' practices and even provide a haven for terrorism.[45] A further staple of such thinking is the proposition that cultural relativism is inexorably undermining enlightenment universalism in the West. As far back as 1988, for instance, French intellectual Alain Finkielkraut argued that:

> The United Nations, founded to propagate the universalist ideal of enlightened Europe, now speaks on behalf of every

ethnic prejudice, believing that peoples, nations and cultures have rights which outweigh the rights of man. The 'multicultural lobby' dismisses the liberal values of Europe as 'racist', while championing the narrow chauvinism of every minority culture.[46]

Countering this attack in a recent study, Will Kymlicka rightly retorts that it amounts to a fundamental misreading of the term multiculturalism as defined in international law. 'The rights of minorities,' Kymlicka insists, 'are an inseparable part of a larger human rights framework and operate within its limits.'[47] Seen in this light, the distinction between national and ethnic minorities is arguably moot. In Kymlicka's view, multiculturalism is about democratization and 'citizenization' – that is to say framing identities within liberal democratic norms and a civil society. By this understanding, giving greater recognition to particular minority communities is a means of increasing their participation in public life and, in so doing, drawing community leaders into fuller interaction with the state and the broader community of which they form part.[48]

In sum, Kymlicka asserts that multiculturalism properly defined challenges both majority *and* minority identities – it does not entrench them. These are sentiments that Renner and Bauer and the liberal activists of the interwar Nationalities Congress would have enthusiastically endorsed. This remains broadly true also of the bigger picture in today's Europe. Between the wars, it has been suggested, liberalism had the appearance of an 'ailing third way in European history'.[49] More than 20 years on from the end of the Cold War, liberalism appears far more entrenched than it did in the late 1920s, even in the face of a pronounced economic crisis that is today severely testing the cohesion and political will of the European Union. Moreover, multiculturalism is presently a far more established fixture on the European political agenda despite the best attempts of various parties to engineer a backlash against it.[50]

By the same token and despite current problems with the common European currency, the contours of the nation state appear less implacably sovereign and 'selfish' than they did in the Europe of the interwar years. Within the EU Schengen area, at least, it is perfectly possible to envisage a longer term scenario whereby state borders do indeed lose much of their practical significance, thereby reducing any perceived conflict of loyalty between transnational ethnic groups and their various states of residence. It is this state of affairs which, ultimately, the interwar Nationalities Congress tried to bring about. In conclusion, while contemporary developments can hardly be characterized as 'Austro-Marxism's last laugh', neither can the debates and practices of the 1920s simply be dismissed as an historical dead end – there is much that can be usefully learned from revisiting them.

Notes

Preface

1 A. Cobban, *The Nation State And National Self-Determination*, London: Fontana, 1969, p. 23.
2 K. Renner, 'State and nation', in E. Nimni (ed.) *National Cultural Autonomy and its Contemporary Critics*, London: Routledge, 2005, p. 32.
3 See D. Christopher Decker, *Enhancing Minority Governance in Romania. Report on the Presentation on Cultural Autonomy to the Romanian Government. ECMI Workshop*, Bucharest, Romania, 3 February 2005, ECMI Report #53. www.ecmi.de/uploads/tx_lfpubdb/Report_53.pdf (downloaded on 22 July 2011).
4 G. Buquicchio, 'Introductory address', in Venice Commission, *The Participation of Minorities in Public Life*, Collection Science and Technique of Democracy, No. 45, Stasbourg, Council of Europe Publishing, 2008, p. 8.

1 Nation, state and minority in modern Europe

1 E. Hobsbawm, *Nations and Nationalism since 1780*, Cambridge: Cambridge University Press, 1990; E. Gellner, *Nations and Nationalism*, Oxford: Blackwell, 1983; G. Schöpflin, *Nations, Identity, Power: The New Politics of Europe*, London: Hurst, 2000; T. Kuzio, ' "Nationalising states" or nation-building? A critical review of the theoretical literature and empirical evidence', *Nations and Nationalism* 7, 2001, pp. 135–154.
2 Here it should be emphasized that the concepts of 'nationhood' and 'national identity' are neither perennial nor static, but historically contingent and contested social and political constructs, the boundaries of which are subject to varying degrees of continuous change and renegotiation within the overall terms of social interaction. As we argue in Chapter 2 of the present work, Karl Renner and Otto Bauer were attuned to this present-day, contingent understanding of the two concepts, which also informs contemporary theories of multiculturalism (see Chapter 7).
3 A. Roshwald, *Ethnic Nationalism and the Fall of Empires: Central Europe, Russia & the Middle East, 1914–1923*, London: Routledge, 2001; A. Webb, *The Routledge Companion to Central and Eastern Europe since 1919*, London: Routledge, 2008.

4 J. Jackson Preece, *National Minorities and the European Nation-States System*, Oxford: Oxford University Press, 1998, pp. 100–101.
5 W. Kymlicka, 'Nation-building and minority rights: comparing West and East', *Journal of Ethnic and Migration Studies*, 26, 2000, pp. 183–212.
6 A. Roshwald, 'Between balkanisation and banalisation: dilemmas of ethno-cultural diversity', in D. J. Smith and K. Cordell (eds) *Cultural Autonomy in Contemporary Europe*, London: Routledge, 2008, pp. 29–42.
7 A. Roshwald, *Ethnic Nationalism*, p. 5; M. Hroch, *Social Preconditions of National Revival in Europe: A Comparative Analysis of the Social Composition of Patriotic Groups among the Smaller European Nations*, Cambridge: Cambridge University Press, 1985; R. Brubaker *et al.*, *Nationalist Politics and Everyday Ethnicity in a Transylvanian Town*, Princeton: Princeton University Press, 2007, pp. 27–46.
8 'A nation is a historically constituted, stable community of people, formed on the basis of a common language, territory, economic life, and psychological make-up manifested in a common culture.' From J. V. Stalin, 'Marxism and the National Question' in J. V. Stalin, *Works*, volume 2, Moscow: Foreign Languages Publishing House, 1954, p. 307; J. Smith, *The Bolsheviks and the National Question, 1917–23*, London: Macmillan, 1999.
9 G. Smith *et al.*, *Nation-Building in the Post-Soviet Borderlands. The Politics of National Identities*, Cambridge: Cambridge University Press, 1998, p. 4; T. Martin, *The Affirmative Action Empire: Nations and National-ism in the Soviet Union, 1923–39*, Ithaca: Cornell University Press, 2001.
10 R. Brubaker, *Nationalism Reframed. Nationhood and the National Question in the New Europe*, Cambridge: Cambridge University Press, 1996, pp. 23–54.
11 For a general overview see ibid., pp. 79–106; R. Pearson, *National Minorities In Eastern Europe, 1848–1944*, London: Macmillan, 1983; Cobban, *Nation State and National Self-Determination*; C. A. MacCart-ney, *National States and National Minorities*, London: Oxford University Press, 1934.
12 E. Berg, 'Ethnic mobilisation in flux: revisiting peripherality and minority discontent in Estonia', *Space and Polity*, 5, 2001, pp. 5–26.
13 Jackson Preece, *National Minorities*, pp. 38–39.
14 For a good overview, see R. Bideleux and I. Jeffries, *A History of Eastern Europe: Crisis and Change*, London: Routledge, 2007, pp. 489–503; Brubaker *et al.*, *Nationalist Politics*, pp. 50–56.
15 Jackson Preece, *National Minorities*, pp. 38–39.
16 S. Bamberger-Stemmann, *Der europäische Nationalitätenkongress 1925 bis 1938*, Marburg: Johann-Gottfried Herder Institut, 2000; M. Rot-barth, 'Grenzrevision und Minderheitenfragen. Zur Funktion des europäischen Minderheiten Kongresses in der Ostpolitik des deutschen Imperialismus', *Studien zur Geschichte der deutsch-polnischen Beziehun-gen*, 6, 1982, pp. 5–30; A. Czubinski, 'La politique d'Allemagne par rapport au minorités nationales allemandes dans les années 1918–1945', *Polish Western Affairs*, 24, 1983, pp. 40–64; R. Michaelson, *Der europäischer Nationalitätenkongress 1925–28. Aufbau, Krise und Konso-lidierung*, Frankfurt: Lang, 1984.
17 See especially E. Nimni (ed.), *National Cultural Autonomy and its Contemporary Critics*, London: Routledge, 2005; also K. Breen and

S. O'Neill (eds), *After the Nation? Critical Reflections on Nationalism and Post-Nationalism*, London: Palgrave, 2010.

18 See, for instance, the discussion in B. Schot, *Nation oder Staat. Deutschland und der Minderheitenschutz*, Marburg: Johann-Gottfried Herder Institut, 1988, pp. 16–17.

19 J. Hiden, *Defender of Minorities. Paul Schiemann, 1876–1944*, London: Hurst, 2004; D. J. Smith, 'Retracing Estonia's Russians: Mikhail Kurchinskii and interwar cultural autonomy', *Nationalities Papers* 27, 1999, pp. 455–474; M. Housden, 'Ewald Ammende and the organisation of national minorities in inter-war Europe', *German History* 18, 2000, pp. 439–460; I. Ijabs, 'Strange Baltic liberalism: Paul Schiemann's political thought revisited', *Journal of Baltic Studies*, 40, 2009, pp. 495–515.

20 Bamberger-Stemmann, *Europäische Nationalitätenkongress.*

21 The most substantial recent study dealing with the origins of cultural autonomy in Estonia is K. Alenius, *Ajan ihanteiden ja historian risitteiden ristipaineissa: Viron etniset suhteet vuosina 1918–1925*, Rovaniemi: Pohjois-Suomen historiallinen yhdistys, 2003. The main points of this book are summarized in K. Alenius, 'Under the conflicting pressures of the ideals of the era and the burdens of history: ethnic relations in Estonia, 1918–1925', *Journal of Baltic Studies* 35, 2004, pp. 32–49. The most comprehensive study in English remains K. Aun, *On the Spirit of the Estonian Minorities Law*, Stockholm: Estonian Information Centre, 1950. Other studies include O. Angelus, *Die Kulturautonomie in Estland*, Detmold: Estnischen Zentralkommittee für Westdeutschland, 1951; K. Aun, *Der Völkerrechtliche Schutz nationaler Minderheiten in Estland von 1917–1940*, Hamburg: Hansischer Gildenverlag, 1951.

22 M. Garleff, 'Autonomiemodellen in den baltischen Staaten zur Zeit ihrer Selbstständigkeit', *Jahrbuch des baltischen Deutschtums*, 1980, pp. 150–156; W. Wachtsmuth, *Von deutscher Arbeit in Lettland 1918–1934: Ein Tätigkeitsbericht. Materialen zur Geschichte des deutschen Deutschtums*, Cologne: Comel Verlag, 1951–1953; Š. Liekis, *A State within a State? Jewish Autonomy in Lithuania 1918–1925*, Vilnius: Versus Aureus, 2003.

23 S. Isakov, *Russkie v Estonii 1918–1940. Istoriko-kul'turniie ocherki*, Tartu: Kompu, 1996; J. Šteimanis, *History of Latvian Jews*, New York: Columbia University Press, 2002; V. Volkovs, *Krievi Latvijā*, Rīga: Latvijas Zinātņu akadēmijas Filozofijas un socioloijas institūta Etnisko pētījumu centrs, 1996; M. Bobe, *Evrei v Latvii*, Riga: Shamir, 2006; S. Isakov (ed.), *Russkoe national'noe men'shinstvo v Estonskoi Respublike (1918–1940)*, Tartu: Kripta, 2000.

24 The most substantial study of the practice of autonomy can be found in Kaido Laurits' work on the German self-government in Estonia during 1925–1940. See: K. Laurits, *Saksa kultuuromavalitsus Eesti Vabariigis 1925–1940.* Tallinn: Rahvusarhiiv, 2008.

2   Voices in the wilderness?

1 In this regard, see also A. Kogan 'The social democrats and the conflict of nationalities in the Habsburg monarchy', *The Journal Of Modern History*, 21, 1949, p. 216.

2 Kogan, 'The social democrats and the conflict of nationalities', pp. 204–217.
3 E. J. Nimni, 'Introduction for the English-reading audience', in O. Bauer, *The Question of Nationalities and Social Democracy*, Minneapolis and London: University of Minnesota Press, 2000, p. xxxv; see also: W. A. Kemp, *Nationalism and Communism in Eastern Europe and The Soviet Union: A Basic Contradiction?* Basingstoke: Macmillan, 1999, p. 36; S. Berger and A. Smith, 'Between Scylla and Charibdis: nationalism, labour and ethnicity across five continents 1870–1939', in S. Berger and A. Smith (eds), *Nationalism, Labour and Ethnicity, 1870–1939*, Manchester: Manchester University Press, 1999, pp. 10–15.
4 Bauer, *The Question of Nationalities and Social Democracy*, pp. 100–102. Here, Bauer differentiates between nationality and class as social categories: the English and German working classes, he argues, are not part of a common 'community of fate', for although they experience the same historical forces, they do not do so in a situation of common reciprocal interaction.
5 Bauer, *The Question of Nationalities and Social Democracy*, pp. 96–106. In this regard, Bauer claimed that, for instance, German culture had determined the character of the Czech nation at a fundamental level; however, the adoption of elements of a foreign culture by a nation never entirely eradicated the difference between the two cultures, it only reduced these differences.
6 'Eine Studie von Dr A. Spindler über die kulturelle Autonomie der völkischen Minoritäten für Vorarbeiten der Autonomie und über die Frage der Volksgemeinschaft', Eesti Riigiarhiiv (ERA) F.85, N.1, S.56.
7 Bauer, *The Question of Nationalities and Social Democracy*, pp. 98–100.
8 This was the case even after the *Ausgleich* of 1867, which had weighted the distribution of power in favour of the German, Magyar and Polish 'historic nations'. Bauer, *The Question of Nationalities and Social Democracy*, pp. 226–230.
9 Ibid., p. 252.
10 Ibid., p. 281.
11 Kogan, 'The social democrats and the conflict of nationalities', pp. 207–212.
12 K. Renner, 'State and nation'.
13 Ibid., p. 20.
14 'Eine Studie von Dr A. Spindler'.
15 See the summary in Bauer, *The Question of Nationalities and Social Democracy*, pp. 284–288. In drawing up this scheme, Renner recognized that no territory was entirely 'nationally homogenous', especially in a context of growing migration. In those instances where local minorities were insufficiently numerous to establish autonomous national delegations, they would be entitled to form autonomous 'concurrences' (*Konkurrenzen*), based on national registers, that would maintain local elementary schools in the relevant language and (in case of need) guarantee members legal assistance when dealing with the local authorities of the canton in question.
16 Ibid.
17 R. Springer (pseudonym of K. Renner), *Grundlagen und Entwicklungsziele der österreichisch-ungarischen Monarchie*, Vienna: 1906, p. 208. Cited in Kogan, 'The social democrats and the conflict of nationalities', p. 214.

18 Bauer, *The Question of Nationalities and Social Democracy*, pp. 287–288.
19 Kogan, 'The social democrats and the conflict of nationalities', p. 213.
20 Bauer, *The Question of Nationalities and Social Democracy*, pp. 274–275.
21 Ibid., p. 290.
22 R. Bauböck, 'Political autonomy or cultural minority rights? A conceptual critique of Renner's model', in E. J. Nimni (ed.), *National Cultural Autonomy and its Contemporary Critics*, p. 99.
23 Kogan, 'The social democrats and the conflict of nationalities', p. 215.
24 J. King, *Budweisers into Czechs and Germans: A Local History of Bohemian Politics, 1848–1948*, Princeton and Oxford: Princeton University Press, 2005, pp. 143–145.
25 Bauer, *The Question of Nationalities and Social Democracy*, pp. 281–283. In this connection, a later author has also noted that 'for all its failings and imperfections,... the Moravian Compromise of 1905 contributed to a considerable easing of the Czech-German ethnic conflict in this crown land', J. Koralka, 'Nationality representation in Bohemia, Moravia and Austrian Silesia, 1848–1914', in G. Alderman (ed.), *Governments, Ethnic Groups and Political Representation*, London: Dartmouth, 1993. Cited in J. Coakley, 'Approaches to the resolution of ethnic conflict: the strategy of non-territorial autonomy', *International Political Science Review*, 15, 1994, p. 312.
26 On Jewish politics within the Tsarist Empire see J. Robinson, 'Die Juden Osteuropas als nationaler Minderheit', *Nation und Staat*, 1 1927, 98ff; E. Mendelsohn, *The Jews of East-Central Europe between the Two World Wars*, Bloomington: Indiana University Press, 1987.
27 For a recent study, see V. Petronis, *Constructing Lithuania: Ethnic Mapping in Tsarist Russia, ca. 1800–1914*, Stockholm: Stockholm University Press, 2007.
28 K. Laurits, *Saksa kultuuromavalitsus Eesti Vabariigis*, p. 45.
29 V. Dohrn, 'State and minorities: the first Lithuanian Republic and S. M. Dubnov's concept of cultural autonomy', in A. Nikzentaitis, S. Schreiner and D. Staliunas (eds), *The Vanished World of Lithuanian Jews*, Amsterdam, and New York: Rodopi, 2004, pp. 155–157; see also Dubnow's letter of 1901, 'Autonomismus als Grundlage eines nationalen Programms', in Simon Dubnow (ed.), *Buch des Lebens. Erinnerungen und Gedanken. Materialien zur Geschichte meiner Zeit, vol. 1 1860–1903*, Göttingen: Vandenhoeck & Ruprecht, 2004, pp. 387ff.
30 V. Dohrn, 'State and minorities', p. 157; A. Verschik, 'The Yiddish language in Estonia: past and present', *Journal of Baltic Studies*, 30, 1999, pp. 117–127; compare also: F. Nesemann, 'Leo Motzkin (1867–1933). Zionist engagement and minority diplomacy', *Central and East European Review*, 1, 2007, pp. 32–54; L. Motzkin, 'Die Konferenz zum Schutz der jüdischen Minderheitsrechte', *Nation und Staat* 1, 1927, 144ff.
31 See the collection of articles in J. von Hehn, H. Von Rimscha and H. Weiss (eds), *Von den baltischen Provinzen zu den baltischen Staaten: Beiträge zur Entstehungsgeschichte der Republiken Estland und Lettland*, Marburg: Johan Gottfried Herder Institut, 1977.
32 E. Thaden (ed.), *Russification in the Baltic Provinces and Finland 1855–1914*, Princeton: Princeton University Press, 1981. There was an

analogous situation in Lithuania, where a polonized nobility had long ruled over an ethnically Lithuanian and Belarussian peasantry and a significant Jewish population. See D. Staliunas, *Making Russians: Meaning and Practice of Russification in Lithuania and Belarus after 1863*, Amsterdam and New York: Rodopi, 2007.

33 G. Von Pistohlkors, 'Führende Schicht oder nationale Minderheit', *Zeitschrift für Ostforschung* 21, 1972, pp. 601–618; A. Ezergailis & G. Pistohlkors (eds), *Die baltischen Provinzen Russlands zwischen den Revolutionen von 1905 und 1917*, Cologne: Boehlau, 1983.

34 P. Schiemann, 'Schlechte Waffen', *Rigasche Rundschau* 1 January 1907.

35 J. King, *Budweisers into Czechs and Germans*, pp. 143–145; W. A. Kemp, *Nationalism and Communism*, p. 42.

36 J. King, *Budweisers into Czechs and Germans*, pp. 209–210.

37 P. Schiemann, 'Die kollektivistische Gefahr', *Rigasche Rundschau*, 18 January 1930.

38 J. V. Stalin, 'Marxism and the National Question', p. 307.

39 R. Brubaker, *Nationalism Reframed*, especially Part II.

40 Quotes from M. H. Boehm, *Europa Irredenta*, Berlin: Hobbing, 1923, pp. 311–312.

41 D. Crols, 'Old and new minorities on the international checkboard: from League to union', in D. J. Smith (ed.), *The Baltic States and their Region: New Europe or Old?* Amsterdam and New York: Rodopi, 2005, pp. 185–209.

42 R. Peters, 'Baltic state diplomacy and the League of Nations minorities system', in J. Hiden and A. Loit (eds), *The Baltic in International Relations between the Two World Wars*, Stockholm: Stockholm university, 1988, pp. 281–302. See also M. Scheuermann, *Minderheitenschutz contra Konfliktverhütung: Die Minderheitenpolitik des Völkerbundes in den zwanziger Jahren*, Marburg: Johann Gottfried Herder-Institut, 2000, pp. 30–48.

43 T. H. Bagley, *General Principles and Problems in the International Protection of Minorities*, Geneva: Imprimeries Populaires, 1950, pp. 89–90.

44 R. Peters, 'Baltic state diplomacy', pp. 293–294.

45 A. Spindler, 'Vähemusrahvuste kultuuriline autonoomia. Gesetzprojekte betreffend die Autonomie deutscher Minderheitgemeinschaft in der Republik Estland. ERA F.55, N.1, S.55 p. 30. On Laun see also S. Salzborn, 'The concept of ethnic minorities. International law and the German-Austrian response', *Behemoth. A Journal on Civilization* 3, 2009, p. 66; G. von Rauch, *The Baltic States. The Years of Independence 1917–1940*, London: Hurst, 1995, p. 141.

46 Quote from Chamberlain's speech to the Council on 9 December, 1925, cited in B. Schot, *Nation oder Staat*, p. 169.

47 E. Ammende, 'Gegen die Entnatsionalisierung – Die These Mello Franco wiederlegt,' *Revaler Bote*, 15 September 1927. Compare, in general, C. Fink, *Defending the Rights of Others: The Great Powers, the Jews and International Minority Protection 1878–1938*, Cambridge: Cambridge University Press, 2004, p. 296ff.

48 Biographical data from Ammende holdings at the *Rossiiskii Gosudarstvennyi Voennyi Arkhiv* (RGVA – Russian State Military Archive), F.1502, O.1, D.30, p. 8.

49 ERA F.1000, N.1, S.137, Deutsch-Baltische Partei in Estland. Organisation und Schutz der nationalen Minoritäten. Ammende to Koch, 26 April 1922.

50 Ibid., p. 2.
51 RGVA F.1502, O.1, D.56. Articles and notes regarding the situation of German minorities in Europe, undated.
52 ERA F.1000, S.137.
53 See for example Paul Schiemann's later reflections on the term, 'Zielsetzung der Minderheiten', in *Der Deutsche in Polen*, 28 June 1936.
54 For a fuller discussion of this difference, see M. Garleff, 'Deutschbaltische Publizisten: Ewald Ammende–Werner Hasselblatt–Paul Schiemann', *Jahrbuch des Bundesinstituts für Ostdeutsche Kultur und Geschichte*, 2, 1994, pp. 189–229.
55 Speech by P. Schiemann to the Congress of European Nationalities, August 1926. *Sitzungsbericht des Kongresses der Organisierten Nationalen Gruppen in den Staaten Europas, Genf, 25 bis 27 August 1926*, Vienna and Leipzig: Willhelm Braumüller, 1927, pp. 34–35.
56 W. Rüdiger, *Aus dem letzten Kapitel deutsch-baltischer Geschichte in Lettland, 1919–1939*, Hannover: Wülflfel, 1955, p. 62.
57 J. Hiden, *Defender of Minorities*, p. 127.
58 'Paul Schiemann scheidet von seinem Werk', *Der Deutsche in Polen*, 29 September 1935. See also Chapter 7 of J. Hiden, *Defender of Minorities*.

3 The Baltic arena

1 A. Ezergailis, *The Holocaust in Latvia*, Riga: Historical Institute of Latvia, 1996, p. 3. Cf. discussion in L. Dribins, 'Die Deutschbalten und die Idee vom nationallettischen Staat 1918–1934', *Nordost-Archiv*, 5, 1996, pp. 277–299. Also V. Volkovs, *Krievi Latvijā*, p. 101.
2 A. Ezergailis, *The Holocaust*, p. 3.
3 B. Mann, *Die baltischen Länder in der deutschen Kriegszielpublizistik 1914–1918*, Tübingen: J. C. B. Mohr, 1965, pp. 121–126. See also V. G. Liulevicius, *War Land on the Eastern Front. Culture, National Identity and German Occupation in World War 1*, Cambridge: Cambridge University Press, 2000, pp. 113–150.
4 J. Tauber and R. Tuchtenhagen, *Vilnius. Kleine Geschichte der Stadt*, Cologne, Weimar, Vienna: Böhlau, 2008, pp. 149–152.
5 J. Tauber, ' "No allies". The Lithuanian *Taryba* and the national minorities 1916–1918', *Journal of Baltic Studies*, 38, 2007, pp. 433–444.
6 See preface to Š. Liekis, *A state within a State*, pp.viii–xi.
7 Ibid., pp. 101–104.
8 See in general H-E. Volkmann, *Die deutsche Baltikumpolitik zwischen Brest-Litovsk und Compiègne*, Cologne: Böhlau, 1970.
9 J. Hiden, *The Baltic States and Weimar Ostpolitik*, Cambridge: Cambridge University Press, 1987, pp. 4–10.
10 P. Schiemann, *Zwischen zwei Zeitaltern. Erinnerungen 1903–1919*, Lüneburg, Nordland-Druck, 1979, pp. 146–149.
11 League of Nations Archive, Geneva (LONA), S.345, N.3, Minorities in Latvia from November 1920 to July 1922.
12 J. Rothschild, *East-Central Europe between the Two World Wars*, Seattle: University of Washington, 1974, p. 377.
13 M. Bobe, *Evrei v Latvii*, p. 161.

14 'Memorandum sur les droits de minorité des juifs en Lettonie addressé au Conseil de la Sociète des Nations par le Comité des delegations Juives', 20 April 1922, LONA S.345, N.3, pp. 20–22.

15 J. Steimanis, *History of Latvian Jews*, p. 71.

16 A. Plakans, *The Latvians. A Short History*, Stanford: Hoover Institution Press, 1995, pp. 126–127.

17 Law for the schooling of minorities in Latvia, 8 December 1919, published in *Valdibas Vestnesis*, Nr 89. See also W. Wachtsmuth, *Von deutscher Arbeit. Vol. 3*, pp. 41ff.

18 See retrospective overview of German schooling by K. Keller, 'Schulen der Minoritäten in Lettland', in Nachlass K. Keller, *Das deutsche Bildungswesen in Lettland 1919–1929*, Johann-Gottfried Herder Insitut, Baltikum, Nr 285.

19 On the minority language provisions of Estonia's schooling laws, see E. Müüripeal, 'Kultuurautonoomia: Eesti Vabariigi vähemusrahvuste haridus- ja keelepoliitika aastail 1981–1940', Magistritöö [master's dissertation], Tallinn: Tallinna Pedagoogikaülikool, 1999, pp. 20–21.

20 K. Alenius, 'Under the conflicting pressures', pp. 35–37.

21 Š. Liekis, *State within a State*, p. 26.

22 J. Hackmann, 'Civil society against the state? Historical experiences of eastern Europe', in J. Hackmann & N. Goetz (eds), *Civil Society in the Baltic Sea Region*, Aldershot: Ashgate, 2003, pp. 57–58.

23 Š. Liekis, *A State within a State*, pp. 131–135.

24 K. Aun, *On the Spirit of the Estonian Minorities Law*, 1949, p. 241.

25 K. Laurits, *Saksa kultuuromavalitsus Eesti Vabariigis*, p. 47.

26 Protocol zasedaniia mandatnoi kommissii S'ezda Evreiskikh Obshchin Estonii, 2 May 1919. ERA F.2297, N.1, S.5.

27 22 March 1921 Letter from the Jewish group to the Deutsch-Baltische Partei in Estland, ERA F.2297, N.1, S.5.

28 K. Alenius, *Ajan ihanteiden ja historian risitteiden ristipaineissa*, p. 335.

29 K. Laurits *Saksa kultuuromavalitsus Eesti Vabariigis*, p. 47.

30 T. Karjahärm and V. Sirk, *Vaim ja võim: Eesti haritlaskond 1917–1940*, Tallinn: Argo, 2001, p. 304.

31 G. von Rauch, *The Baltic States*, p. 141.

32 T. Karjahärm and V. Sirk, *Vaim ja võim*, pp. 304–305.

33 See the intervention by Ado Anderkopp to the parliamentary debate on cultural autonomy in 1923. Cited in *I Riigikogu Protokollid 9 istungjärk 1923a., protokollid Nr 185–221* (Tallinn: kirjatuse o-ü "täht" trükk Tallinnas), p. 2075.

34 K. Alenius, *Ajan ihanteiden ja historian risitteiden ristipaineissa*, pp. 329–330.

35 Speech by *Riigikogu* member W. Ernits (Social Democrat) on 1 January 1923, *I Riigikogu Protokollid 9 istungjärk 1923a., protokollid Nr 185–221*, p. 2053.

36 Ibid., p. 2068.

37 Ibid., p. 2062.

38 Ibid., p. 2046–2047.

39 'Die Debatten im Kulturrat über die Frage der Verwirklichung der kulturellen Selbstverwaltung', *Revaler Bote*, 5 November 1925.

40 Stackelberg to Hasselblatt, 27 December 1924, ERA F.1000, N.1, S.172. Deutsch-Baltische Partei in Estland. Korrespondenz des Abgeordneten W. Hasselblatt November 1921 to January 1925.
41 M. Garleff, *Deutschbaltische Politik zwischen den Weltkriegen*, Bonn-Bad Godesburg: wissenschaftliche Archiv, 1976, p. 106.
42 Ibid., pp. 106–107; *Revaler Bote*, 13 December 1921.
43 Eine Studie von Dr A. Spindler über die kulturelle Autonomie der völkischen Minoritäten.
44 Ibid.
45 Ibid.
46 Ibid.
47 Cited in K. Laurits, *Saksa kultuuromavalitsus Eesti Vabariigis*, p. 30.
48 M. Garleff, *Deutschbaltische Politik*, p. 107.
49 'Gesetz-Projekt über die zeitweilige Ordnung der Selbstverwaltung der nationalen Minderheiten', *Revaler Bote*, 2 March 1923.
50 LONA, R 1665–27181, 'Discussion au parlement Esthonien sur le projet de loi relative à l'autonomie des minorités en Esthonie; A. Heyking, *The Main Issues Confronting the Minorities of Latvia and Estonia*, London: 1922.
51 *I Riigikogu Protokollid 9 istungjärk 1923a*, *protokollid Nr 185–221*, pp. 2050–2052.
52 For one example, 'Deutsche Schulhilfe in Estland im Jahre 1924', in *Baltische Blätter*, 24 February 1924. See also deputy Max Bock's remark on the subject, *I Riigikogu Protokollid 9 istungjärk 1923a.*, *protokollid Nr 185–221*, pp. 2076–2077.
53 K. Alenius, *Ajan ihanteiden ja historian risitteiden ristipaineissa*, p. 334.
54 'Auf dem Wege zur Kulturautonomie', *Revaler Bote*, 22 March 1924; see also K. Alenius, *Ajan ihanteiden ja historian risitteiden ristipaineissa*, p. 335.
55 'Die erste Lesung des Autonomie-Gesetzes', *Revaler Bote*, 7 June 1924.
56 'Staatsversammlung', *Revaler Bote*, 5 April 1924.
57 *I Riigikogu protokollid 9 istungjärk protokol Nr 114 (17)*, pp. 951ff.
58 Avtonomia natsional'nykh men'shinstv', *Posledniia Izvestiia*, 18 January 1925.
59 See the arguments in J. Hiden, *Defender of Minorities*, pp. 99ff.
60 In a recent analysis of Schiemann's political thought, Ivars Ijabs argues that his liberalism was derived from German romanticism rather than from the Western Enlightenment currents embodied by the likes of Locke and Bentham. In this regard, Ijabs maintains, Schiemann remained convinced of the superiority of German culture and the importance of a German cultural mission in the Baltic (Ijabs, 'Strange Baltic liberalism', p. 502). The fact remains, however, that throughout his career Schiemann was a staunch advocate both of the Republic of Latvia and of the national rights not only of Latvians, but of all other ethnic groups living within the country's borders.
61 Paul Schiemann to Nikolai von Berg, 14 January 1923, Schiemann Nachlass. Nikolai von Berg 1922–1936, Baltijas Centrala Biblioteka, Riga.
62 For a general overview, see P. Schiemann, 'Die nationalen Minderheiten in Lettland', *Zeitschrift für Politik*, 14, 1925, 276–281.
63 In general, see M. Bobe, *Evrei v Latvii*, pp. 200–201; E. Mendelsohn, *The Jews of East-Central Europe*, pp. 241ff; M. Garleff, 'Ethnic minorities in

the Estonian and Latvian parliaments: the politics of coalition', in V. S. Vardys and R. J. Misiunas (eds), *The Baltic States in Peace and War 1917–1945*, Philadelphia and London: The Pennsylvania State University Press, 1978, pp. 81–94.
64 M. Bobe, *Evrei v Latvii*, pp. 200–201.
65 Ibid., p. 219.
66 J. Hiden, *Defender of Minorities*, pp. 97ff.
67 Protocol of the meeting of the German Democratic Party, 1 December 1925. Latvijas Valsts Vēsture Archīvs (LVVA) F.4985, A.1, L.4.
68 Ibid.
69 Ibid.
70 Ibid.
71 In general, see W. Wachtsmuth, *Von deutscher Arbeit in Lettland 1918–1934. Vol. 1.*

4 The practice of autonomy

1 K. Laurits, *Saksa kultuuromavalitsus*, p. 70.
2 *Revaler Bote*, 6 May 1925.
3 See undated memorandum by Hasselblatt 'Leitsätze zum Referat über innere Organisationsprobleme des Deutschtums'. RGVA F.1502, O.1, D.111, p. 59.
4 K. Laurits, *Saksa kultuuromavalitsus*, pp. 70–71.
5 'Saksa wähemusrahvuse kultuur-autonoomia', *Vaba Maa*, 8 August 1925; Vorbereitender Arbeitsausschuss f. die deutsche Kulturautonomie -Wählen zum 1 Deutsch-Estländischen Kulturrat. ERA F.85, N.1, S.2.
6 Nottbeck to Schultz 2 May 1925. ERA F. 85, N.1, S.4.
7 'Endised "kadakad" wälja', *Vaba Maa*, 23 July 1925.
8 Protokolle des 1 deutschen Kulturrats 1 November 1925–22 October 1928 Nr 13 21/22 October 1928. F.85, N.1, S.66.
9 Vorbereitender Arbeitsausschuss f. die deutsche Kulturautonomie -Wählen zum 1 Deutsch-Estländischen Kulturrat. ERA F.85, N.1, S.2.
10 Nottbeck to Krueger, 5 May 1925 and Nottbeck letter of 14 May 1925. Vorbereitender Arbeitsausschuss f. die deutsche Kulturautonomie, Wählen zum 1 Deutsch-Estländischen Kulturrat. ERA F.85, N.1, S.4.
11 Circular from Hasselblatt. Vorbereitender Arbeitsausschuss f. die deutsche Kulturautonomie – Wählen zum 1 Deutsch-Estländischen Kulturrat. F85, N.1, S.4.
12 Note by Nottbeck, early August 1925. ERA F.85, N.1, S.4; see also K. Laurits, *Saksa kultuuromavalitsus* pp. 27, 71–72. In their response to the questionnaire distributed to them by Ewald Ammende, German leaders insisted that the findings of the 1922 census did not correspond to reality, in so far as 16,000 people had voted for the Deutsch-Baltische Partei in Estland in the May 1923 elections. By this reckoning they estimated the real German population to be as high as 30,000 Fragebogen IV. RGVA F.1502, O.1, D.63, p. 64.
13 Kirjavahetus isikutega rahvuse muutmise kohta. ERA F.14., N.1, S.1127.
14 'Saksa wähemusrahvuse kultuur-autonoomia', Nottbeck to Schultz 2 May 1925. ERA F. 85, N.1, S.4..
15 K. Laurits, *Saksa kultuuromavalitsus*, p. 71, citing E. Madisson, *Die nationalen Minderheiten Estlands und ihre Rechte*, Tallinn: Tallinna

Eesti Kirjastus-Ühisuse trükikoda, 1926, p. 21. Undated memo early 1925. Vortbereitender Arbeitsausschuss f. die deutsche Kulturautonomie -Wählen zum 1 Deutsch-Estländischen Kulturrat. ERA F.85, N.1, S.2.

16 O. Hartger, 'Brauchen wir ein neues Wahlsystem für die Kulturratswahlen?' *Revaler Bote* 8 August 1929; see also S. Klau, 'Der Entwurf des neuen Kulturratswahlrechts', *Revalsche Zeitung*, 14 November 1930.

17 K. Laurits, *Saksa kultuuromavalitsus*, p. 72.

18 'Die kulturelle Selbstverwaltung wird werwirklicht', *Baltische Blätter*, 15 November 1925.

19 Ibid.

20 Ibid.

21 Estnische Übersetzungen der Protokolle des I Kulturrats. 1 Nov. 1925–22 Okt 1928: I. Eesti saksa kultuurnõukogu avamise koosoleku 1 Nov 1925 mustapeade klubis Tallinnas. Protokoll no. 1. ERA F.85, N.1, S.67.

22 Ibid.

23 Ibid.

24 Ibid.

25 Protokolle des 1 deutschen Kulturrats 1 November 1925–22 October 1928 Nr 3, 10 November 1925. ERA F.85, N.1, S.66.

26 'Die Arbeit der Deutschenkulturverwaltung im Jahre 1925–26', *Revaler Bote*, 20 November 1926.

27 *Riigi Teataja* (1918, 75/76: 593).

28 See report by Harry Koch appended to Protokolle des 1 deutschen Kulturrats 1 November 1925–22 October 1928 Nr 13 21/22 October 1928. ERA F.85, N.1, S.66.

29 'Stellungnahme der Stadt zum Unterhalt der deutschen Schulen,' *Revaler Bote*, 4 November 1926.

30 Report by Koch in Protokolle des 1 deutschen Kulturrats 1 November 1925–22 October 1928, Nr 9. ERA F.85, N.1, S.66.

31 Protokolle des 1 deutschen Kulturrats 1 November 1925–22 October 1928 Nr 3, 10 November 1925. ERA F.85, N.1, S.66; see also 'Zur Steuer der Deutschenkulturselbstverwaltung', *Revaler Bote*, 22 October 1926.

32 Protokolle des 1 deutschen Kulturrats 1 November 1925–22 October 1928 Nr 5, 14 March 1926. ERA F.85, N.1, S.66.

33 Protokolle des 1 deutschen Kulturrats 1 November 1925–22 October 1928. Meeting of 28–29 November 1927; ERA F.85, N.1, S.66, p. 142.

34 Hasselblatt to Bruns, 11 April 1928. Deutsch-Baltische Partei in Estland. Briefe von Dr Bruns 1924–9. ERA F.1000, N.1, S.170.

35 Protokolle des II Deutschen kulturrats 9 Dec. 1928–13 Sept. 1931. ERA F.85, N.1, S.78, p. 142.

36 Š. Liekis, *A State within a State?*, pp. 135–136.

37 Protokolle des 1 deutschen Kulturrats, 1 November 1925–22 October 1928, Nr 3, 10–11 November 1925. F.85, N.1, S.66.

38 Protokolle des 1 deutschen Kulturrats, 1 November 1925–22 October 1928, Nr 10, 4 July 1927. F.85, N.1, S.66, p. 10.

39 Protokolle des 1 deutschen Kulturrats, 1 November 1925–22 October 1928, Nr 12, 25 June 1928. F.85, N.1, S.66.

40 See, for instance, A. de Vries 'Zehn Jahre Verband Deutscher Vereine in Estland,' *Revalsche Zeitung*, 27 September 1930.

41 Denkschrift zur Frage der Behandlung der Nationalitäten in Deutschland mit besonderer Rücksicht auf die Rückwirkung auf das bodenständige europäische Auslandsdeutschum, 28 October 1924. RGVA F.1502, O.1, D.110.

42 'Von der Tätigkeit der Gesellschaft "Deutsche Schulhilfe" in Estland', *Revaler Bote*, 23 April 1924.

43 *Revaler Bote*, 17 March 1926; 'Herbsttagung des deutschen Kulturrats in Estland', *Baltische Blätter*, 3 July 1927; H. Pantenius, 'Zur Frage eines Netzes unserer deutschen Schulen', *Revaler Bote*, 21 July 1927.

44 Protokolle des 2 deutschen Kulturrats 9 Dec. 1928–13 Sept. 1931, Protokoll Nr 1, 9–10 December 1928. ERA F.85, N.1, S.78.

45 Protokolle des 1 deutschen Kulturrats, 1 November 1925–22 October 1928, Nr 12, 25 June 1928. F.85, N.1, S.66.

46 Ibid.

47 Ibid.

48 Protokolle des 2 deutschen Kulturrats, 9 Dec. 1928–13 Sept. 1931, Nr 5, 16 March 1930. ERA F.85, N.1, S.78.

49 Protokolle des 2 deutschen Kulturrats, 9 Dec. 1928–13 Sept. 1931, Nr 8, 13 September 1931. ERA F.85, N.1, S.78.

50 Protokolle des 2 deutschen Kulturrats, 9 Dec. 1928–13 Sept. 1931, Nr 6, 23 November 1930. ERA F.85, N.1, S.78; see also 'Zu den bevorstehenden Veränderung im deutschen Schulwesen', *Revalsche Zeitung*, 14 November 1930.

51 S. Klau, 'Der Entwurf des neuen Kulturratwahlrechts'.

52 Ibid.

53 The new arrangements were duly accepted at the spring meeting of the second German Cultural Council on 22 March 1931. See 'Zur Tagung des deutschen Kulturrats', *Revalsche Zeitung*, 20 March 1931.

54 'Protokolle des 1 deutschen Kulturrats, 1 November 1925–22 October 1928', Nr 13, 22 October 1928. ERA F.85, N.1, S.66. See also the concerns expressed in the responses to Ammende's earlier questionnaire. RGVA F.1502, O.1, D.63.

55 Tagebuch des Schulrats no. 2 1928–1929. ERA F.85, N.2, S.685.

56 Protokolle des 1 deutschen Kulturrats, 1 November 1925–22 October 1928, Nr 13, 22 October 1928, Nr 10, 4 July 1927. ERA F.85, N.1, S.66.

57 Ibid.

58 See Denkschriften und Berichten, W. Wachtsmuth, 'Die rechtlichen Grundlagen des deutschen Schulwesens in Lettland.' Undated memo probably written early 1933. LVVA F.2125, A.2, L.12.

59 J. Šteimanis, *History of Latvian Jews*, p. 184; M. Bobe, *Evrei v Latvii*, pp. 218–226.

60 Izglitibas Ministrija Ebreju Izglitibas Parvalde Fonda 1920–1934g. Parvaldes padomes sežu protokoli 1920.g. (Ministry of Education Jewish Section 1920–1934. Minutes of meetings of the Council of the Section 1920), LVVA F.2125, A.4, L.29.

61 Minutes of meetings of the Council of the Russian Section of the Ministry of Education 24 January 1924 to 2 September 1932. LVVA, F.2125, A.1, L.45, pp. 25–26. Of the remaining pupils in the secondary schools,

214 were Latvian, 124 German and the rest a combination of Belorussian, Polish, Lithuanian, Estonian and other nationalities. Of 1,403 pupils at 18 private elementary schools, meanwhile, 799 were Jewish, 431 Russian, 80 Latvian, 44 German, 21 Polish and 28 of other nationalities.

62 LVVA F.2125, A.4, L.29, p. 4.
63 Minutes of meetings on 26 April 1920 and 29 August 1920. LVVA F.2125, A.4, L.29, pp. 8, 14.
64 Minutes of meeting of 26 April 1920. LVVA F.2125, A.4, L.29, p. 8.
65 Ibid. In this regard it is perhaps significant that Landau himself ran a Russian-language school in Riga.
66 M. Bobe, *Evrei v Latvii*, p. 197.
67 Ibid., p. 224.
68 K. Laurits, *Saksa kultuuromavalitsus*, p. 67.
69 A. Verschik, 'The Yiddish language in Estonia: past and present', pp. 119–120.
70 Ibid., p. 121.
71 Kirjavahetus Juudi Kultuurvalitsuse ja koolivalitsustega õppekeele valiku küsimuses juudi koolides, tunnikavade kinnitamise ja välismaistele õppejõududele elamis- ja teenistusloa saamise, koolide toetuste saamise, õppealalistes, koolide Juudi Vähemusrahvuse Kultuuromavalitsuse Koolivalitsusele. ERA F.1108, N.3, S.616, p. 99.
72 Ibid., p. 32.
73 Ibid., p. 46.
74 Ibid., p. 76.
75 Ibid., p. 66.
76 Ibid., p. 141.
77 For an overview, see S. Isakov, *Russkie v Estonii 1918–1940*; V. Volkovs, *Krievi Latvijā*; D. J. Smith, 'Retracing Estonia's Russians'; S. Isakov (ed.), *Russkoe National'noe Men'shinstvo v Estonskoi Respublike*.
78 D. J. Smith, 'Retracing Estonia's Russians', p. 461.
79 Ibid., pp. 465–466.
80 Ibid.
81 Ibid., p. 461.
82 Ibid., p. 462; see also Ü. Rajasalu, 'Russkie v Estonii 1918–1940. Obshchii obzor', in S. Isakov (ed.), *Russkoe National'noe Men'shinstvo v Estonskoi Respublike*, pp. 21–61.
83 M. Krabbe, 'L'autonomie culturelle comme solution du problème des minorités. Note de M.Krabbe au date du 18 Nov 1931'. LONA R.2175–4–32835; see also *Posledniie Izvestiia*, 10 May 1925.
84 V. Boikov, S. Isakov and Ü. Rajasalu 'Politicheskaia Zhizn', in S. Isakov, *Russkoe National'noe Men'shinstvo v Estonskoi Respublike*, p. 69.
85 D. J. Smith, 'Retracing Estonia's Russians', p. 465.
86 Ibid.
87 Minutes and circulars of the National Democratic Union. LVVA F.5645, A.1, L.3. The National Democratic Union was renamed the *Russkoe Natsional'noe Ob'edinenie* from the start of 1924.
88 V. Volkovs, *Krievi Latvijā*, pp. 104–105.
89 Minutes of meetings of the Council of the Russian Section of the Ministry of Education, 24 January 1924–2September 1932. LVVA F.2125, A. 1, L.45, p. 19.

90 Ibid., p. 45.
91 LVVA F.5645, A.1, L.3, pp. 62–65.
92 See P. Schiemann 'Die vereitelte Minderheitenfront', *Rigasche Rund-schau*, 30 October 1926.
93 V. Volkovs, *Krievi Latvijā*, p. 102.
94 A. Purs, 'The price of free lunches: making the frontier Latvian in the interwar years,' *Global Review of Ethnopolitics* 1, 2002, pp. 60–73.
95 'Antwort auf die Fragen, wie sich das Mehrheitsvolk zu der Minderheiten-frage gestellt hat, und welchen Standpunkt die vershiedenen Minderheiten zu ihr einnehmen' Nachlass K. Keller. Das deutsche Bildungswesen in Lett-land 1919–1929. Herder Institut Baltikum Nr 285.
96 Ibid.
97 Protokolle des 1 deutschen Kulturrats, 1 November 1925–22 October 1928, Nr 13, 22 October 1928. ERA F.85, N.1, S.66; see also H. Koch, 'Das Estlandische Deutschtum 1918–1930', *Revalsche Zeitung*, 29 Sep-tember 1930.
98 A. de Vries, 'Fünf Jahre Deutsche Kulturselbstverwaltung,' *Revalsche Zeitung*, 22 November 1930; Ewald Ammende's opening remarks to the VII Congress of European Nationalities, Geneva, 29th–31st August 1931, LONA R2161–4–31096–3817.
99 Ewald Ammende's opening remarks.
100 V. Volkovs, *Krievi Latvijā*, pp. 102–104.
101 Cited in D. J. Smith, 'Retracing Estonia's Russians,' 466.

5 Nationalities in congress

1 RGVA F.1502, O.1, D.22.
2 'Die Minderheiten. P. Schiemann über die Ergebnisse des Genfer-Kongresses,' *Rigasche Rundschau*, 4 September 1926.
3 *Sitzungsbericht des Kongresses der Organisierten Nationalen Gruppen in den Staaten Europas, Genf, 29 bis 31. August 1928*, Vienna and Leipzig: Willhelm Braumüller, 1928, pp. 29–31.
4 S. Bamberger-Stemmann, *Der europäische Nationalitätenkongress*, p. 86ff.
5 J. Hiden, *Defender of Minorities*, pp. 110ff.
6 Memorandum cited in B. Schot, *Nation oder Staat*, p. 147.
7 Ibid.; on critics of Stresemann compare B. Schot, *Stresemann, der deut-sche Osten und der Völkerbund*, Wiesbaden: Zabern, 1984, and M. Rot-barth, 'Grenzrevision und Minderheitenfragen', 10ff.
8 B. Schot, *Nation oder Staat*, p. 147.
9 Compare the discussion at the *Verband* conference of 21 July 1924. 'Deutsch-Baltische Partei in Estland. Völkerbund und Minderheitenfra-gen. ERA F., N.1, S.142.
10 Entwurf W. H. 1924/5 Deutsch-Baltische Partei in Estland. Briefe von Dr Bruns 1924–9. ERA F.1000, N.1, S.170.
11 S. Bamberger-Stemmann, *Der europäische Nationalitätenkongress*, p. 91ff. For Ammende's account of the origins of the Congress, see: letter from E. Ammende to Marckutti 22 December 1925, RGVA F.1502, O.1, D.26, pp. 147–152.
12 One was held in Vienna (1932), one in London (1937) and one in Stock-holm (1938).

13 S. Bamberger-Stemmann, *Der europäischen Nationalitätenkongress,* p. 111.

14 M. Garleff, 'Baltische Minderheitenvertreter auf den europäischen Nationalitätenkongressen 1925–1938', *Jahrbuch des baltischen Deutschtums,* 1986, p. 119.

15 Resolutions of the European Nationalities Congress. RGVA F.1502, O.1, D.113, pp. 34–35.

16 Interview between George Popoff, Geneva correspondent of the *Rigasche Rundschau* and P. Schiemann, 'Die Minderheiten. P. Schiemann über die Ergeibnisse des Genfer-Kongresses,' *Rigasche Rundschau,* 4 September 1926.

17 Minutes of the Committee of German Balt Parties 5 November 1925, LVVA F.4985, A.1, L.4.

18 From file of Ammende's post-Congress correspondence with newspaper editors. RGVA F.1502, O.1, D.27, p. 5.

19 Ibid., p. 8.

20 Ibid., p. 2.

21 See for example E. Ammende, 'Die Sprache der Zahlen,' *Nation und Staat* 10/11, 1931, pp. 650–656.

22 S. Bamberger-Stemman, *Der Europäische Nationalitätenkongress,* pp. 421–422; see also 'Minderheiten und interparlamentarische Union', *Revalsche Zeitung,* 26 July 1930.

23 Cf. P. Schiemann, 'Minoritätenschutz und Nationalitätenrecht', *Rigasche Rundschau,* 20 February 1926.

24 P. Schiemann, 'Heilige Rechte', *Rigasche Rundschau,* 22 December 1928.

25 G. Stresemann, 'Die Minderheitenfrage als Friedensproblem', *Kölnische Volkszeitung. Sonderbeilage,* 1 August 1929.

26 Ibid.

27 Report on 1931 Minorities Congress, 29–31 August, LONA R2161–4–31096–3817, p. 5.

28 LONA R2175–4–32835, p. 1.

29 See discussion in C.-G. Bruns 'Genfer Nationalitätenkongress', *Auslandswarte* 17–18, 1927. Nachlass Bruns, Herder Institut Marburg DSHI 100 Bruns.

30 P. Schiemann, 'Die Spaltung im Nationalitätenkongress', *Nation und Staat* 1, 3 (1927/8), pp. 158–70.

31 P. Schiemann, 'Nationalitäten-kongress', *Rigasche Rundschau,* 12 September 1931.

32 P. Schiemann, 'Streitfragen der Nationalitätenkongress', *Rigasche Rundschau,* 1 October 1927.

33 S. Bamberger-Stemman, *Der europäischer Nationalitätenkongress,* pp. 176–177.

34 'Soveshchanie predstavitelei russkikh men'shinstv' 6 goudarstv' v rige', *Segodnia* 232, 22 August 1929; 'Die erstmalige Tagung der russischen Minderheiten', *Nation und Staat,* 1 Oktober 1929, pp. 73–74; 'Deiatel'nost' russkago natsional'nago soyuza za 1929 goda (otchet')' LVVA F.2666, A.1, L.3, pp. 93–96.

35 'Die erstmalige Tagung der russischen Minderheiten'; 'Soveshchanie predstavitelei russkikh men'shinstv''.

36 Ibid.

37 L. Krabbe, 'L'autonomie culturelle'.
38 Ibid.
39 Ibid.
40 Ibid.
41 Ibid.
42 'Pessimismus und Optimismus. Rede von Dr. P. Schiemann, gehalten auf dem Nationalitätenkongress in Genf,' *Rigasche Rundschau*, 5 September 1931.
43 P. Schiemann, 'Coudenhove und Rohan,' *Nation und Staat*, 10/11, 1930, pp. 630–636; M. Kurchinskii, *Soedinennie shtati Evropy: ekonomicheskie I politicheskie perspektivy etoi idei*, Tartu: Tartu Ülikooli toimetused, 1930.
44 See Ludvig Krabbe's report on the 8th Congress of European Nationalities, 29 June 1932, LONA R2161–37541.
45 P. Schiemann, *'Die neue nationalistische Welle'*. The original manuscript for this is in the Schiemann Nachlass, Baltijas Centrale Biblioteka, Riga. Drei Manuskripte 1932–1939, no. 1. For an English-language translation, see *Central and East European Review*, 1, 2007 http://spaces.brad.ac.uk:8080/display/ssishistoryjournal (downloaded on 6 July 2010).
46 Ibid.
47 See letters Ammende to Schiemann on 6, 14 and 19 March 1931 in Schiemann Nachlass: Volksgr ENK korresp. 1929–30.
48 P. Schiemann, *'Die neue nationalistische Welle'*.
49 Ibid.
50 A full account of the controversy is contained in S. Bamberger-Stemmann, *Der europäische Nationalitätenkongress*, pp. 278 ff. H. Glass, 'Die Deutsch-judische Kontroverse auf dem europäischen Nationalitätenkongress,' unpublished paper presented at the Simon Dubnow Institute, Leipzig, 2005 as part of the project 'Jewish diplomacy, minority rights and human rights – the exertion of Jewish influence and the formation of international law 1919–1948'; see also F. Nesemann, 'Leo Motzkin (1867–1933): Zionist engagement and minority diplomacy'.
51 S. Bamberger-Stemmann, *Der europäische Nationalitätenkongress*, pp. 275 ff.
52 Ibid.
53 H. Glass, 'Die Deutsch-Jüdische Kontoverse'.
54 P. Schiemann, 'Dissimilation und Nationalitätenrechte' Dokumente aus dem politischen Nachlass von Hans Otto Roth 1919–1951. Nr 232 pp. 420–424. Draft text of speech that Schiemann had intended to deliver at the Berne meeting of the Nationalities Congress on 16–19 September 1933. Kindly made available to the authors by Dr Hildrun Glass.
55 H. Glass, 'Die Deutsch-Jüdische Kontoverse'.
56 Ibid; S. Bamberger-Stemmann, *Der europäische Nationalitätenkongress*, pp. 275–278.
57 H. Glass, 'Die Deutsch-Jüdische Kontoverse'.
58 *Sitzungsbericht des Kongresses der Organisierten Nationalen Gruppen in den Staaten Europas, Bern, 16 bis 18. September 1933* (Vienna and Leipzig: Willhelm Braumüller, 1934), p. 23; 'Men'shinstvennyi kongress trebuet organizatsii mezhdunarodnoi pomoshchi golodayushchim v SSSR', *Segodniia*, September 1933.

59 'Nechego razgovarivat' ob uchastii v men'shinstvennom kongresse – zayavlyaet dep M. Dubin', *Segodniia*, September 1933.
60 H. Glass, 'Die Deutsch-Jüdische Kontoverse'.
61 *Sitzungsbericht des Kongresses der Organisierten Nationalen Gruppen in den Staaten Europas, Bern, 16 bis 18. September 1933*, p. 98.
62 Ibid., pp. 70–71. Different interpretations could be placed upon Kurchinskii's intervention in this debate. On the one hand, the declaration is suggestive of a commitment to upholding the rights of all minorities. However, the refusal to name Nazi Germany is at odds with his earlier willingness to explicitly condemn the policies of the USSR in Ukraine, which contravened the rules of the Congress. Also, unlike Paul Schiemann, Kurchinskii continued to participate in the Congress after 1933, at a time when the organization was quite obviously under the sway of national socialism. Was then the 1933 declaration simply a tokenistic one, on the part of an individual for whom anti-communism was the paramount motivating force? For a fuller comparison of Schiemann, Kurchinkii and Ammende, see M. Housden and D. J. Smith, 'A matter of uniqueness? Paul Schiemann, Ewald Ammende and Mikhail Kurchinskii compared', in M. Housden and D. J. Smith, *Forgotten Pages in Baltic History. Diversity and Inclusion*, Amsterdam and New York: Rodopi, 2011, pp. 161–86.
63 Wilfan to Schiemann, 20 February 1934. Nachlass Schiemann. Volksgruppen 1933–1935.
64 Ammende to Schiemann 10 July 1934. Nachlass Schiemann. Volksgruppen 1933–1935.
65 'Paul Schiemann scheidet von seinem Werk', *Der Deutsche in Polen*, 29 September 1935.

6 The new nationalist wave

1 P. Schiemann, 'Das Herr in Lettland', *Rigasche Rundschau*, 1 August 1931.
2 P. Schiemann, 'Einheitskultur', *Rigasche Rundschau*, 9 January 1932.
3 Schiemann's report to Deutschbaltische Demokratische Partei, 9 February 1932, LVVA F.4985, A.1, L.5.
4 W. Wachtsmuth, 'Eine Bilanz der Schulpolitik des Ministers Kehnisch', LVVA F.2125, A.2, L.12, Denkschriften und Berichte; Minutes of Meetings of the Council of the Russian Dept of the Ministry of Education from 24 January 1924 to 2 September 1932 LVVA F.2125, A.1, L.45.
5 'Minorités en Lettonie 1932', LONA S.345, No. 532 (10).
6 Ibid.
7 L. Dribins, 'Die Deutschbalten und die Idee vom nationallettischen Staat'.
8 P. Schiemann, 'Hüben und Drüben,' *Rigasche Rundschau*, 30 January 1932.
9 'Die Unvollkommenheit unserer Kulturselbstverwaltung', *Revaler Bote*, 5 April 1929.
10 'Estland. Gesetz uber Änderung der Nationalität', *Nation und Staat*, 2 November 1928, p. 142.
11 'Abbau im Mittelschulnetz', *Revalsche Zeitung*, 23 July 1931.
12 Kirjavahetus Saksa Kultuurvalitsusega ja isikutega saksa vähemusrahvuse koolide õppejõudude koosseisu, õpperaamatute kirjastamise loa muretsemise, segaabieludest sündinud laste koolitamise asjus ja teistes õppealalisis küsimusis; õppekavad ja õpilaste nimestikud 02.05.1932–11.12.1936, ERA F.1108, N.3, S.202, pp. 116–117.

13 A further five pupils at the school were Russian by nationality. Ibid., p. 140.
14 ERA F.1108, N.3, S.202, pp. 23, 94.
15 Schiemann to Nikolai von Berg 21 December 1931, Nachlass Schiemann. Nikolai von Berg-Paul Schiemann 1922–1936.
16 ERA F.1108, N.3, S.202, p. 340.
17 ERA F.1108, N.3, S.202, 2 May 1932–11 December 1936.
18 Schiemann to Winkler 9 February 1933. Nachlass Schiemann. Rigasche Rundschau Briefe no. 221–48.
19 *Baltische Monatshefte*, February 1933.
20 Die Lage – Estland, *Nation und Staat*, Heft 8, May 1934, pp. 521–523.
21 K. Laurits, *Saksa kultuuromavalitsus*, pp. 87–88.
22 G. von Rauch, *The Baltic States*, p. 154.
23 A.-M. Köll, *Peasants on the World Market: Agricultural Experience of Independent Estonia, 1919–1939*, Stockholm: University of Stockholm, 1994, p. 111.
24 On minority ownership of businesses see T. Pärming, 'The Jewish community. Inter-ethnic relations in Estonia, 1918–1940', *Journal of Baltic Studies*, 10, 1979, pp. 241–262.
25 Cited by I. Feldmanis, 'Die Deutschbalten: ihre Einstellung zum Nationalsozialismus und ihr Verhältnis zum Staat Lettlands 1933–1939', *Nordost-Archiv 5*, 1996, p. 383.
26 On credit restrictions in Latvia, cf. Bank of England Report of 13 November 1933: 'Latvia'. Bank of England Archive OV118/Latvia.
27 Cited in I. Butulis, 'Die Deutschbalten in der Lettischen Presse in den Jahren 1930–1934', *Nordost-Archiv 5*, 1996, pp. 315–316.
28 See J. Šteimanis, *History of Latvian Jews*.
29 See for example the overview of Karl Keller, 'Die deutsche Parlamentsfraktion' (Juli 1919–Mai 1934), Nachlass Keller, Herder Institute, Baltikum 288.
30 Ibid., p. 177.
31 Memorandum of 18 July 1934, Die Auswirkungen des neuen Volsbildungsgesetzes auf das deutsche Schulwesen in Lettland. LVVA F.2125, A.2, L.12, Denkschriften und Berichte.
32 V. Volkovs, *Krievi Latvijā*, p. 102.
33 ERA F.1108, N.3, S.202, p. 301, citing *Riigi Teataja*, 105, 1934.
34 Letter from the German cultural government to the Riigivanem, 24 April 1934, ERA F.1108, N.3, S.202, p. 207.
35 ERA F.1108, N.3, S.202, p. 301.
36 Ibid.
37 Ibid.
38 See G. von Rauch, *The Baltic States*, p. 170.
39 Ü. Rajasalu, 'Russkie v Estonii 1918–1940', p. 40.
40 Ibid., p. 42.
41 'Zehn Jahre deutsche Kulturselbstverwaltung', *Nation und Staat*, January 1936, pp. 222–226.
42 'Die Lage. Estland. Die neue Verfassung-Vorbereitungen zu den Wahlen', *Nation und Staat*, Jan. 1938, pp. 9, 240ff.
43 Ibid. Also, Ü. Rajasalu, 'Russkie v Estonii 1918–1940', p. 47.
44 Estnische Übersetzungen der Protokolle des IV Kulturrats 8 April 1934–26 March 1939, p. 27, meeting of 7 November 1937, ERA F.85, N.1, S.96.

45 Estnische Übersetzungen der Protokolle des IV Kulturrats 8 April 1934–26 March 1939 appendix 1 to minutes of meeting on 29/3/36, pp. 67–68, ERA F.85, N.1, S.96.
46 G. von Rauch, *The Baltic States*, p. 171.
47 Ü. Rajasalu, 'Russkie v Estonii 1918–1940', pp. 42–43.
48 Ibid., p. 42.
49 In this respect see M. Ketola, *The Nationality Question in the Estonian Evangelical Lutheran Church, 1918–1939*, Helsinki: Finnish Society of Church History, 2000.
50 Cited in J. von Hehn, *Die Umsiedlung der baltischen Deutschen – das letzte Kapitel baltish-deutscher Geschichte*, Marburg/Lahn: Herder-Institut, 1982, p. 167.
51 Ibid., p. 166.
52 P. Schiemann, 'Ich warne', *Rigasche Rundschau*, 12 March 1920.
53 P. Schiemann, Die Umsiedlung 1939 und die europäischer Minderheiten-politik, unpublished manuscript written in Riga in spring 1940. Subsequently reprinted in *Jahrbuch des baltischen Deutschtums* 21, 1974, p. 105.
54 E. Hobsbawm, *The Age of Extremes: The Short Twentieth Century, 1914–1991*, London: Michael Joseph, 1994. On the demise of democracy and emergence of ethnic violence in interwar Eastern Europe see also: A. Prusin, *The Lands Between: Conflict in the East European Borderlands, 1870–1992*, Oxford and New York: Oxford University Press, 2010.
55 On these events, see O. Mertelsmann with A. Rahi-Tamm, 'Soviet mass violence in Estonia revisited,' *Journal of Genocide Research* 11, 2009, pp. 307–322.
56 J. Hiden, *Defender of Minorities*, pp. 240–251.
57 J. Hackmann, 'Werner Hasselblatt. Von der estländischen Kulturautonomie zur nationalsozialistischen Bevölkerungspolitik', in M. Garleff (ed.), *Deutschbalten, Weimarer Republik und Drittes Reich*, Cologne, Weimar and Vienna: Böhlau, 2008, pp. 71–107. The extent to which Ewald Ammende might have colluded with the actions of the Nazi regime in occupied Eastern Europe can only be guessed at, as the Nationalities Congress general secretary – long in poor health – died of a stroke in 1936 during a trip to China. Similarly, Mikhail Kurchinskii died of a heart attack in Estonia in June 1939, just a couple of months before he would have been confronted with the dilemma of whether to join the Baltic German *Umsiedlung*. See Housden and Smith, 'A matter of uniqueness?'.
58 See V. Freimane, *Ardievu Atlantīda!* Riga: Atēna, 2011; V. Freimane 'Remembering Paul Schiemann,' *Journal of Baltic Studies*, 31, 2000, pp. 432–437. Compare Schiemann's reaction to the prospect of war in asking 'Ende der Nationalitätenbewegung?' in *Der Deutsche in Polen*, 9 April 1939, where he reaffirms the need for maintaining the principles of the European nationalities movement.

7 Cultural autonomy – a new chapter?

1 For full text see www.conventions.coe.int (downloaded on 13 September 2010).
2 See for instance the introduction to R. G. Suny and T. Martin (eds), *A State of Nations: Empire and Nation Making in the Age of Lenin and Stalin*, Oxford: Oxford University Press, 2001.

3 W. Kymlicka, *Multicultural Odysseys: Navigating the New International Politics of Diversity*, Oxford and New York: Oxford University Press, 2007, p. 3.

4 See R. Kaiser, 'Nationalism and identity', in M. Bradshaw (ed.), *Geography and Transition in the Post-Soviet Republics*, Chichester: J. Wiley & Sons, 1997, pp. 9–30.

5 See G. Smith (ed.), *The Nationalities Question in the Post-Soviet States*, London: Longman, 1996.

6 In general see R. Brubaker, *Nationalism Reframed*.

7 See O. Ieda (ed.), *Beyond Sovereignty: from Status Law to Transnational Citizenship*, Sapporo: Hokkaido University, 2006.

8 A. Roshwald, 'Between balkanization and banalization', p. 31.

9 D. Chandler, 'The OSCE and the internationalisation of national minority rights', in K. Cordell (ed.), *Ethnicity and Democratisation in the New Europe*, London: Routledge, 1999, pp. 61–76.

10 Witness the claim in 1999 by then OSCE High Commissioner Max van der Stoel that 'insufficient attention has been given to the possibilities of cultural autonomy.' M. Van der Stoel, *Peace and Stability through Human and Minority Rights: Speeches by the OSCE High Commissioner on National Minorities*, Baden Baden: Nomos Verlagsgesellschaft, 1999, p. 172.

11 W. Kymlicka, 'National cultural autonomy and international minority rights norms', in D. Smith and K. Cordell (eds), *Cultural Autonomy*, pp. 43–57; also W. Kymlicka, 'Nation building and minority rights'.

12 See the report on the proceedings of the Venice Commission, *The Participation of Minorities in Public Life*. Collection science and technique of democracy, Number 45, Strasbourg: Council of Europe Publishing, 2008.

13 On Smith and Hiden's briefing see D. C. Decker, 'Enhancing minority governance in Romania: Report on the presentation on cultural autonomy to the Romanian government', European Centre for Minority Issues Report, Number 53, March 2005. http://www/ecmi.de/download/Report_53.pdf (downloaded 13 September 2010).

14 C. Codagnone and V. Filippov, 'Equity, exit and national identity in a multi-national federation: "the multi-cultural consitutional patriotism" project in Russia', *Journal of Ethnic and Migration Studies* 26, 2000, pp. 263–288. Also V. Tolz, *Russia: Inventing the Nation*, London: Arnold, 2001, pp. 249–256.

15 Tolz, *Russia: Inventing the Nation*, p. 251.

16 B. Bowring, 'Burial and resurrection: Karl Renner's controversial influence on the "national question" in Russia', in E. Nimni (ed.), *National Cultural Autonomy and its Contemporary Critics*, London: Routledge, 2005, p. 201.

17 Ibid., p. 203. See also B. Bowring, 'Austro-Marxism's last laugh? The struggle for recognition of national cultural autonomy for Rossians and Russians', *Europe Asia Studies* 54, 2002, pp. 229–250.

18 D. J. Smith, 'Cultural autonomy in Estonia. A relevant paradigm for the post-Soviet era?' ESRC One Europe or Several? Working paper 19/01, 2001.

19 'Eestirootslased taastavad kultuurilise omavalitsuse', *Postimees*, 2 February 2007.

20 D. J. Smith, 'Cultural autonomy in Estonia'.

21 E. Kekelidze, 'Eto budet estonskii variant', *Estoniia*, 18 September 1992.
22 See for instance, I. Katz, 'Avtonomiia – delo dobrovol'noe', *Stolitsa*, 1 December 2008. Also, 'Seifulen: venelaste kultuurilise autoonomia teket pärsivad omavahelised erimeelsused', *Eesti Päevaleht*, 29 December 2009.
23 D. C. Decker, 'The use of cultural autonomy to prevent conflict and meet the Copenhagen criteria: the case of Romania', in D. Smith and K. Cordell (eds), *Cultural Autonomy*, pp. 101–114.
24 A. Krizsán, 'The Hungarian minority protection system: a flexible approach to the adjudication of ethnic claims', *Journal of Ethnic and Migration Studies* 26, 2000, pp. 247–62. See also A. Pap, 'Minority rights and diaspora claims: collision, interdependence and loss of orientation', in O. Ieda (ed.), *Beyond Sovereignty*, pp. 243–248.
25 B. Dobos, 'The development of cultural autonomy in Hungary', *Ethnopolitics* 6, 2007, pp. 451–469.
26 Ibid. See also A. Krizsán, 'The Hungarian minority protection system'.
27 M. Kovacs, 'The good, the bad and the ugly: three faces of "dialogue" – the development of Roma politics in Hungary', *Contemporary Politics* 3, 1997, pp. 55–71; M. Kovacs, 'The political significance of the first national gypsy minority self-government in Hungary', *Contemporary Politics* 6, 2000, pp. 247–262.
28 B. Dobos, 'The development of cultural autonomy in Hungary'.
29 I. Klimova-Alexander, 'Transnational Romani and indigenous non-territorial self-determination claims', in D. J. Smith and K. Cordell (eds), *Cultural Autonomy*, pp. 59–80.
30 S. Deets, 'Pulling back from neo-medievalism: the domestic and international politics of the Hungarian status law', in O. Ieda, *Beyond Sovereignty*, pp. 17–36.
31 Ibid.
32 B. Majtény, 'Utilitarianism in minority protection? Status laws and international organizations', in O. Ieda (ed.), *Beyond Sovereignty*, pp. 3–16.
33 J. Coakley, 'Approaches to the resolution of ethnic conflict', p. 310; on the Belgian model, see also J.-C. Scholsem, 'Personal autonomy through the "communities system": does the example of Belgium suggest that forms of non-territorial autonomy can make a difference in terms of minority participation?" in Venice Commission, *The Participation of Minorities in Public Life*, pp. 101–118.
34 On immigrant multiculturalism, see *inter alia* W. Kymlicka, *Politics in the Vernacular: Nationalism, Multiculturalism and Citizenship*, Oxford and New York: Oxford University Press, 2001.
35 Kymlicka, 'National cultural autonomy and international minority rights norms', p. 46.
36 See in this regard S. Vertovec and S.Wessendorf, 'Introduction: assessing the backlash against multiculturalism in Europe', in S. Vertovec and S. Wessendorf (eds), *The Multiculturalism Backlash*, London and New York: Routledge, 2010, p. 23, where it is noted how 'since the 1950s, the construction of difference and diversity in Britain has moved from concerns with "race" during the 1950s and 1960s, to discussions surrounding "ethnicity", then "culture" and then "faith"'. This is discussed more fully by R. Grillo, 'Britain and others: from "race" to "faith"' in the same volume, pp. 50–71.

37 C. Clarke, 'Royal Commonwealth Society speech November 15th, 2006', copy supplied to the authors by Charles Clarke.

38 Taken from www.archbishopofcanterbury.org/articles.php/1135/sharia-law-what-did-the-archbishop-actually-say (downloaded 26 July 2011).

39 Ibid. For full text, see www.archbishopofcanterbury.org/articles.php/1137/archbishops-lecture-civil-and-religious-law-in-england-a-religious-perspective (downloaded 26 July 2011).

40 See, in this respect, the vigorous debate engendered on the discussion website Socialist Unity by Andy Newman's article 'Otto Bauer and contemporary questions of multiculturalism', which sought to link the Williams debate to the earlier ideas of the Austro-Marxists. www.socialistunity.com/?p=1874 (downloaded 23 March 2011).

41 www.archbishopofcanterbury.org/articles.php/1135/sharia-law-what-did-the-archbishop-actually-say (downloaded 26 July 2011).

42 See the discussion in Grillo, 'British and others: from "race" to "faith"', pp. 61–2.

43 See Vertovec and Wessendorf (eds), *The Multiculturalism Backlash*.

44 W. Kymlicka, 'The rise and fall of multiculturalism?: New debates on inclusion and accommodation in diverse societies', in S. Vertovec and S. Wessendorf (eds), *The Multiculturalism Backlash*, pp. 32–33.

45 S. Vertovec and S. Wessendorf, 'Introduction: assessing the backlash against multiculturalism in Europe', in S. Vertovec and S. Wessendorf (eds), *The Multiculturalism Backlash*, London and New York: Routledge, 2010.

46 A. Finkielkraut, *The Undoing of Thought*, London: Claridge Press, 1998, cited in W. Kymlicka, *Multicultural Odysseys*, p. 6.

47 W. Kymlicka, *Multicultural Odysseys*, p. 7.

48 W. Kymlicka, 'The rise and fall of multiculturalism?', pp. 32–49.

49 N. Davies, *Europe East and West*, London: Pimlico, 2007, p. 19.

50 W. Kymlicka, 'The rise and fall of multiculturalism?', pp. 40–43.

Archival references

Estonian State Archive (testi Riigiarhiiv ERA)

F.14, N.1, S.1127: Kirjavahetus isikutega rahvuse muutmise kohta.

F.55, N.1, S.55: Vähemusrahvuste kultuuriline autonoomia. Gesetzprojekte betreffend die Autonomie deutscher Minderheitgemeinschaft in der Republik Estland.

F.85, N.1, S.2: Vorbereitender Arbeitsausschuss f. die deutsche Kulturautonomie-Wählen zum 1 Deutsch-Estländischen Kulturrat.

F.85, N.1, S.56: 'Eine Studie von Dr A. Spindler über die kulturelle Autonomie der völkischen Minoritäten für Vorarbeiten der Autonomie und über die frage der Volksgemeinschafts.

F.85, N.1, S.66: Protokolle des 1 deutschen Kulturrats 1 November 1925–22 October 1928 Nr 13, 21/22 October 1928.

F.85, N.1, S.67: Estnische Übersetzungen der Protokolle des I Kulturrats. 1 Nov. 1925–22 Okt 1928: I. Eesti saksa kultuurnõukogu avamise koosoleku 1 Nov 1925 mustapeade klubis Tallinnas. Protokoll no. 1.

F.85, N.1, S.78: Protokolle des 2 deutschen Kulturrats, 9 Dec. 1928–13 Sept. 1931, Nr 8, 13 September 1931.

F.85, N.1, S.96: Estnische Übersetzungen der Protokolle des IV Kulturrats 8 April 1934–26 March 1939.

F.1000, N.1, S.137: Deutsch-Baltische Partei in Estland. Organisation und Schutz der nationalen Minoritäten.

F.1000, N.1, S.170: Deutsch-Baltische Partei in Estland. Briefe von Dr Bruns 1924–9.

F.1000, N.1, S.142: Deutschbaltische Partei in Estland. Völkerbund und Minderheitenfragen.

F.1000, N.1, S.172: Deutsch-Baltische Partei in Estland. Korrespondenz des Abgeordneten W. Hasselblatt.

F.1108, N.3, S.202: Kirjavahetus Saksa Kultuurvalitsusega ja isikutega saksa vähemusrahvuse koolide õppejõudude koosseisu, õpperaamatute kirjastamise loa muretsemise, segaabieludest sündinud laste koolitamise asjus ja teistes õppealalisis küsimusis; õppekavad ja õpilaste nimestikud 2.5.1932–11.12.1936.

F.1108, N.3, S.616: Kirjavahetus Juudi Kultuurvalitsuse ja koolivalitsustega õppekeele valiku küsimuses juudi koolides, tunnikavade kinnitamise ja

välismaistele õppejõududele elamis- ja teenistusloa saamise, koolide toetuste saamise, õppealalistes, koolide Juudi Vähemusrahvuse Kultuuromavalitsuse Koolivalitsusele.
F.2297, N.1, S.5: Protocol zasedaniia mandatnoi kommissii S'ezda Evreiskikh Obshchin Estonii, 2 May 1919.

League of Nations Archive, Geneva (LONA)

S.345, N.3: Minorities in Latvia from November 1920 to July 1922.
S.345, N.3: Memorandum sur les droits de minorité des juifs en Lettonie addressé au Conseil de la Socièté des Nations par le Comité des delegations Juives, 20 April 1922.
R.1665–27181: 'Discussion au parlement Esthonien sur le projet de loi relative à l'autonomie des minorités en Esthonie'.
R.2175–4–32835: M. Krabbe, 'L'autonomie culturelle comme solution du problème des minorités'. Note de M.Krabbe au date du 18 Nov 1931.
R.2161–4–31096–3817: Ewald Ammende's opening remarks to the VII Congress of European Nationalities, Geneva, 29th–31st August 1931.
R.2161–4–31096–3817: Report on 1931 Minorities Congress, 29–31 August.
R.2161–37541: Ludvig Krabbe's report on the 8th Congress of European Nationalities, 29 June 1932.

Russian State Military Archive – Moscow (Rossiiskii Gosudarstvennyi Voennyi Arkhiv – RGVA)

F.1502, O.1, D.30: Biographical data from Ammende holdings.
F.1502, O.1, D.56: Articles and notes regarding the situation of German minorities in Europe, undated.
F.1502, O.1, D.63: Fragebogen IV.
F.1502, O.1, D.111: Undated memorandum by Hasselblatt 'Leitsätze zum Referat über innere Organisationsprobleme des Deutschtums'.
F.1502, O.1, D.110: Denkschrift zur Frage der Behandlung der Nationalitäten in Deutschland mit besonderer Rücksicht auf die Rückwirkung auf das bodenständige europäische Auslandsdeutschum, 28 October 1924.
F.1502, O.1, D.113: Resolutions of the European Nationalities Congress.

Johann-Gottfried Herder Institut – Marburg

Baltikum, Nr 285: Nachlass K. Keller. Das deutsche Bildungswesen in Lettland 1919–1929: Schulen der Minoritäten in Lettland.
Baltikum, Nr 285: Nachlass K. Keller. Das deutsche Bildungswesen in Lettland 1919–1929: Die deutsche Parlamentsfraktion (Juli 1919–Mai 1934).
Baltikum 288: Nachlass Keller: Antwort auf die Fragen, wie sich das Mehrheitsvolk zu der Minderheitenfrage gestellt hat, und welchen Standpunkt

die vershiedenen Minderheiten zu ihr einnehmen.
DSHI 100 Bruns. Nachlass Bruns. Genfer Nationalitätenkongress (1927).

Latvian State History Archive (Latvijas Valsts Vēstures Arhīvs – LVVA)

F.2125, A.4, L.29: Izglitibas Ministrija Ebreju Izglitibas Parvalde Fonda 1920–1934g. Parvaldes padomes sežu protokoli 1920.g.

F.2125, A.1, L.45: Minutes of meetings of the Council of the Russian Section of the Ministry of Education 24 January 1924 to 2 September 1932.

F.2125, A.2, L.12: Denkschriften und Berichte, W. Wachtsmuth. Eine Bilanz der Schulpolitik des Ministers Kehnisch.

F.2125, A.2, L.12: Denkschriften und Berichte, W. Wachtsmuth. Memorandum of 18 July 1934. Die Auswirkungen des neuen Volsbildungsgesetzes auf das deutsche Schulwesen in Lettland.

F.2125, A.2, L.12: Denkschriften und Berichten, W. Wachtsmuth: Die rechtlichen Grundlagen des deutschen Schulwesens in Lettland.

F.2666, A.1, L.3: Deiatel'nost' russkago natsional'nago soyuza za 1929 goda (otchet').

F.4985, A.1, L.4: Protocol of the meeting of the German Democratic Party, 1 December 1925.

F.4985, A.1, L.5: Deutschbaltische Demokratische Partei, 9 February 1932.

F.5645, A.1, L.3: Minutes and circulars of the National Democratic Union.

Baltijas Centrālā Bibliotēka, Riga

Schiemann Nachlass. Nikolai von Berg 1922–1936.
Schiemann Nachlass. Rigasche Rundschau Briefe no. 221–248.
Schiemann Nachlass. Volksgr ENK Korresp. 1929–30.

Bank of England Archive

OV118/Latvia

Bibliography

Alenius, K., *Ajan ihanteiden ja historian risitteiden ristipaineissa: Viron etniset suhteet vuosina 1918–1925*, Rovaniemi: Pohjois-Suomen historiallinen yhdistys, 2003.

Alenius, K., 'Under the conflicting pressures of the ideals of the era and the burdens of history: ethnic relations in Estonia, 1918–1925', *Journal of Baltic Studies* 35, 2004, pp. 32–49.

Ammende, E., 'Gegen die Entnationalisierung – Die These Mello Franco wiederlegt', *Revaler Bote*, 15 September 1927.

Ammende, E., 'Die Sprache der Zahlen', *Nation und Staat* 10/11, 1931.

Angelus, O., *Die Kulturautonomie in Estland*, Detmold: Estnischen Zentralkommittee für Westdeutschland, 1951.

Archbishop of Canterbury, www.archbishopofcanterbury.org/articles.php/1135/sharia-law-what-did-the-archbishop-actually-say (downloaded 26 July 2011).

Archbishop of Canterbury, www.archbishopofcanterbury.org/articles.php/1137/archbishops-lecture-civil-and-religious-law-in-england-a-religious-perspective (downloaded 26 July 2011).

Aun, K., *On the Spirit of the Estonian Minorities Law*, Stockholm: Estonian Information Centre, 1950.

Aun, K., *Der Völkerrechtliche Schutz nationaler Minderheiten in Estland von 1917–1940*, Hamburg: Hansischer Gildenverlag, 1951.

Bagley, T. H., *General Principles and Problems in the International Protection of Minorities*, Geneva: Imprimeries Populaires, 1950.

Bamberger-Stemmann, S., *Der europäische Nationalitätenkongress 1925 bis 1938*, Marburg: Johann-Gottfried Herder Institut, 2000.

Bauböck, R., 'Political autonomy or cultural minority rights? A conceptual critique of Renner's model', in Nimni, E. (ed.), *National Cultural Autonomy and its Contemporary Critics*, London: Routledge, 2005.

Bauer, O., *The Question of Nationalities and Social Democracy*, Minneapolis and London: University of Minnesota Press, 2000.

Berg, E., 'Ethnic mobilisation in flux: revisiting peripherality and minority discontent in Estonia', *Space and Polity* 5, 2001, pp. 5–26.

Berger, S. and Smith, A. (eds), *Nationalism, Labour and Ethnicity, 1870–1939*, Manchester: Manchester University Press, 1999.

Berger, S. and Smith, A., 'Between Scylla and Charibdis: nationalism, labour and ethnicity across five continents 1870–1939', in Berger and Smith (eds.), *Nationalism, Labour and Ethnicity, 1870–1939*, Manchester: Manchester University Press, 1999.

Bideleux, R. and Jeffries, I., *A History of Eastern Europe: Crisis and Change*. London: Routledge, 2007.

Boehm, M.-H., *Europa Irredenta*, Berlin: Hobbing, 1923.

Boikov, V., Isakov, S. and Rajasalu, Ü., 'Politicheskaia Zhizn', in Isakov, S. (ed.), *Russkoe national'noe men'shinstvo v Estonskoi Respublike (1918–1940)*, Tartu: Kripta, 2000, pp. 62–98.

Bradshaw, M. (ed.), *Geography and Transition in the Post-Soviet Republics*, Chichester: J. Wiley and Sons, 1997.

Breen, K. and O' Neill, S. (eds.), *After the Nation? Critical Reflections on Nationalism and Post-Nationalism*, London: Palgrave, 2010.

Brubaker, R., *Nationalism Reframed. Nationhood and the National Question in the New Europe*, Cambridge: Cambridge University Press, 1996.

Brubaker, R., Feischmidt, M. and Fox, J., *Nationalist Politics and Everyday Ethnicity in a Transylvanian Town*, Princeton: Princeton University Press, 2007.

Bobe, M., *Evrei v Latvii*, Riga: Shamir, 2006.

Bowring, B., 'Austro-Marxism's last laugh? The struggle for recognition of national cultural autonomy for Rossians and Russians', *Europe-Asia Studies* 54, 2002, pp. 229–250.

Bowring, B., 'Burial and resurrection: Karl Renner's controversial influence on the "national question" in Russia', in Nimni, E. (ed.), *National Cultural Autonomy and its Contemporary Critics*, London: Routledge, 2005, pp. 191–206.

Butulis, I., 'Die Deutschbalten in der Lettischen Presse in den Jahren 1930–1934', *Nordost-Archiv* 5, 1996, pp. 301–324.

Buquicchio, G., 'Introductory address', in *Venice Commission: The Participation of Minorities in Public Life*, Collection Science and Technique of Democracy, No. 45, Stasbourg, Council of Europe Publishing, 2008, p. 8.

Chandler, D., 'The OSCE and the internationalisation of national minority rights,' in Cordell, K. (ed.), *Ethnicity and Democratisation in the New Europe*, London: Routledge, 1999, pp. 61–76.

Clarke, C., 'Royal Commonwealth Society speech November 15th, 2006', copy supplied to the authors by Charles Clarke.

Coakley, J., 'Approaches to the resolution of ethnic conflict: the strategy of non-territorial autonomy', *International Political Science Review* 15, 1994, pp. 297–314.

Cobban, A., *The Nation State and National Self-Determination*, London: Fontana, 1969.

Codagnone, C. and Filippov, V., 'Equity, exit and national identity in a multi-national federation: "The multi-cultural consitutional patriotism" project in Russia', *Journal of Ethnic and Migration Studies* 26, 2000, pp. 263–288.

Cordell, K. (ed.), *Ethnicity and Democratisation in the New Europe*, London: Routledge, 1999.

Crols, D., 'Old and new minorities on the international checkboard: from league to union', in D. J. Smith, *The Baltic States and their Region: New Europe or Old?*, Amsterdam and New York: Rodopi, 2005, pp. 185–209.

Czubinski, A., 'La politique d'Allemagne par rapport au minorités nationals allemandes dans les années 1918–1945', *Polish Western Affairs* 24, 1983, pp. 40–64.

Davies, N., *Europe East and West*, London: Pimlico, 2007.

Decker, D. C., *Enhancing Minority Governance in Romania. Report on the Presentation on Cultural Autonomy to the Romanian Government*. ECMI *Workshop*, Bucharest, Romania, 3 February 2005, ECMI Report # 53. www.ecmi.de/uploads/tx_lfpubdb/Report_53.pdf (downloaded on 22 July 2011).

Decker, D. C., 'The use of cultural autonomy to prevent conflict and meet the Copenhagen criteria: the case of Romania', in Smith, D. J. and Cordell, K. (eds), *Cultural Autonomy in Contemporary Europe*, London: Routledge, 2008, pp. 101–114.

Deets, S., 'Pulling back from neo-medievalism: the domestic and international politics of the Hungarian status law', in Ieda, O. (ed.), *Beyond Sovereignty: from Status Law to Transnational Citizenship*, Sapporo: Hokkaido University, 2006, pp. 17–36.

De Vries, A., 'Zehn Jahre Verband Deutscher Vereine in Estland', *Revalsche Zeitung*, 27 September 1930.

De Vries, A., 'Fünf Jahre Deutsche Kulturselbstverwaltung,' *Revalsche Zeitung*, 22 November 1930.

Dobos, B., 'The development of cultural autonomy in Hungary', *Ethnopolitics* 6, 2007, pp. 451–469.

Dohrn, V., 'State and minorities: the first Lithuanian Republic and S.M. Dubnov's concept of cultural autonomy', in Nikzentaitis, A., Schreiner, S. and Staliunas, D, (eds), *The Vanished World of Lithuanian Jews*, Amsterdam, and New York: Rodopi, 2004, pp. 155–173.

Dribins, L., 'Die Deutschbalten und die Idee vom nationallettischen Staat 1918–1934', *Nordost-Archiv*, Neue Folge, 5, 1996, pp. 277–299.

Dubnow, S. (ed.), *Buch des Lebens. Erinnerungen und Gedanken. Materialien zur Geschichte meiner Zeit, vol. 1, 1860–1903*, Göttingen: Vandenhoeck & Ruprecht, 2004.

Ezergailis, A., *The Holocaust in Latvia*, Riga: Historical Institute of Latvia, 1996.

Ezergailis, A. and Pistohlkors, G. (eds), *Die baltischen Provinzen Russlands zwischen den Revolutionen von 1905 und 1917*, Cologne: Boehlau, 1983.

Feldmanis, I., 'Die Deutschbalten: ihre Einstellung zum Nationalsozialismus und ihr Verhältnis zum Staat Lettlands 1933–1939', *Nordost-Archiv* 5, 1996, pp. 363–386.

Fink, C., *Defending the Rights of Others: the Great Powers, the Jews and International Minority Protection 1878–1938*, Cambridge: Cambridge University Press, 2004.

Finkielkraut, A., *The Undoing of Thought*, London: Claridge Press, 1998.

Freimane, V., 'Remembering Paul Schiemann', *Journal of Baltic Studies* 31, 2000, pp. 432–437.

Freimane, V., *Ardievu Atlantīda!* Riga: Atēna, 2011.

Garleff, M., *Deutschbaltische Politik zwischen den Weltkriegen*, Bonn-Bad Godesburg: wissenschaftliche Archiv, 1976.

Garleff, M., 'Ethnic minorities in the Estonian and Latvian parliaments: the politics of coalition', in Vardys, V. S. and Misiunas, R. J. (eds), *The Baltic States in Peace and War 1917–1945*, Philadelphia and London: The Pennsylvania State University Press, 1978, pp. 81–94.

Garleff, M., 'Autonomiemodellen in den baltischen Staaten zur Zeit ihrer Selbstständigkeit', *Jahrbuch des baltischen Deutschtums*, 1980, pp. 150–156.

Garleff, M., 'Baltische Minderheitenvertreter auf den europäischen Nationalitätenkongressen 1925–1938', *Jahrbuch des baltischen Deutschtums*, 1980, pp. 117–131.

Garleff, M., 'Deutschbaltische Publizisten: Ewald Ammende–Werner Hasselblatt–Paul Schiemann', *Jahrbuch des Bundesinstituts für Ostdeutsche Kultur und Geschichte* 2, 1994, pp. 189–229.

Gellner, E., *Nations and Nationalism*, Oxford: Blackwell, 1983.

Glass, H., 'Die Deutsch-judische Kontroverse auf dem europäischen Nationalitätenkongress', unpublished paper presented at the Simon Dubnow Institute, Leipzig, 2005, as part of the project 'Jewish diplomacy, minority rights and human rights – the exertion of Jewish influence and the formation of international law 1919–1948'.

Grillo, R., 'Britain and others: from "race" to "faith"', in Vertovec, S. and Wessendorf, S. (eds), *The Multiculturalism Backlash*, London and New York: Routledge, 2010, pp. 50–71.

Hackmann, J., 'Civil society against the state? Historical experiences of Eastern Europe', in Hackmann, J. and Goetz, N. (eds), *Civil Society in the Baltic Sea Region*, Aldershot: Ashgate, 2003, pp. 49–62.

Hackmann, J., 'Werner Hasselblatt. Von der estländischen Kulturautonomie zur nationalsozialistischen Bevölkerungspolitik,' in Garleff, M. (ed.), *Deutschbalten, Weimarer Republik und Drittes Reich*, Cologne, Weimar and Vienna: Böhlau, 2008, pp. 71–107.

Hackmann, J. and Goetz, N. (eds), *Civil Society in the Baltic Sea Region*, Aldershot: Ashgate, 2003.

Hartger, O., 'Brauchen wir ein neues Wahlsystem für die Kulturratswahlen?', *Revaler Bote*, 8 August 1929.

Heyking, A., *The Main Issues Confronting the Minorities of Latvia and Estonia*, London, 1922.

Hiden, J., *The Baltic States and Weimar Ostpolitik*, Cambridge: Cambridge University Press, 1987.

Hiden, J., *Defender of Minorities. Paul Schiemann, 1876–1944*, London: Hurst, 2004.

Hiden, J., 'Adolf Köster und Paul Schiemann in Riga', in Angermann, N.,

Garleff, M. and Lenz, W. (eds), *Ostseeprovinzen, Baltische Staaten und das Nationale*, Münster: Lit Verlag, 2005, pp. 447–457.

Hiden, J., 'Propagatiang the anational state'. Paul Schiemann's concept of minority rights', in *Simon-Dubnow-Institut Yearbook*, Göttingen: Vandenhoek & Ruprecht, 2005, pp. 99–109.

Hiden, J., 'Die Ideen Paul Schiemanns über Nation und Staat', in Garleff, M. (ed.), *Deutschbalten, Weimarer Republik und Drittes Reich*, Cologne, Weimar, Vienna: Böhlau Verlag, 2008, pp. 109–120.

Hiden, J., 'Das Konzept der Minderheitenrechte in Europa. Eine vergessene Stimme aus Lettlands Vergangenheit', in Müller-Plantenburg, C. and Perels, J. (eds), *Kritik eines technokratischen Europa. Der politische Widerstand und die Konzeption einer europäischen Verfassung*, Kassel: Universität Kassel, 2008, pp. 71–80.

Hiden, J., 'Paul Schiemann: Anwalt der Minderheiten', in Henning, D. (ed.), *Nationale und ethnische Konflikte in Estland und Lettland während der Zwischenkriegszeit*, Lüneburg: Carl-Schirren-Gesellschaft e.V., 2009, pp. 137–155.

Hiden J. and Loit A. (eds), *The Baltic in International Relations between the Two World Wars*, Stockholm: University of Stockholm, 1988.

Hobsbawm, E., *Nations and Nationalism since 1780*, Cambridge: Cambridge University Press, 1990.

Hobsbawm, E., *The Age of Extremes: The Short Twentieth Century, 1914–1991*. London: Michael Joseph, 1994.

Housden, M., 'Ewald Ammende and the organisation of national minorities in inter-war Europe', *German History* 18, 2000, pp. 439–460.

Housden, M. and Smith, D. J., 'A matter of uniqueness? Paul Schiemann, Ewald Ammende and Mikhail Kurchinskii compared', in Housden, M. and Smith, D. J., *Forgotten Pages in Baltic History. Diversity and Inclusion*, Amsterdam and New York: Rodopi, 2011, pp. 161–186.

Housden, M. and Smith, D. J., *Forgotten Pages in Baltic History. Diversity and Inclusion*, Amsterdam and New York: Rodopi, 2011.

Hroch, M., *Social Preconditions of National Revival in Europe: A Comparative Analysis of the Social Composition of Patriotic Groups among the Smaller European Nations*, Cambridge: Cambridge University Press, 1985.

Ieda, O. (ed.), *Beyond Sovereignty: from Status Law to Transnational Citizenship*, Sapporo: Hokkaido University, 2006.

Ijabs, I., 'Strange Baltic liberalism: Paul Schiemann's political thought revisited', *Journal of Baltic Studies* 40, 2009, pp. 495–515.

I Riigikogu Protokollid 9 istungjärk 1923a., protokollid Nr 185–221, Tallinn: kirjatuse o-ü "täht" trükk Tallinnas.

Isakov, S., *Russkie v Estonii 1918–1940. Istoriko-kul'turniie ocherki*, Tartu: Kompu, 1996.

Isakov, S. (ed.), *Russkoe national'noe men'shinstvo v Estonskoi Respublike (1918–1940)*, Tartu: Kripta, 2000.

Jackson Preece, J., *National Minorities and the European Nation-States System*, Oxford: Oxford University Press, 1998.

Kaiser, R., 'Nationalism and identity', in Bradshaw, M. (ed.), *Geography and Transition in the Post-Soviet Republics*, Chichester: J. Wiley and Sons, 1997, pp. 9–30.

Karjahärm, T. and Sirk, V., *Vaim ja võim: Eesti haritlaskond 1917–1940*, Tallinn: Argo, 2001.

Katz, I., 'Avtonomiia – delo dobrovol'noe', *Stolitsa*, 1 December 2008.

Kekelidze, E., 'Eto budet Estonskii variant', *Estoniia*, 18 September 1992.

Keller, K., 'Schulen der Minoritäten in Lettland', in Nachlass K. Keller, *Das deutsche Bildungswesen in Lettland 1919–1929*, Johann-Gottfried Herder Insitut, Baltikum.

Kemp, W. A., *Nationalism and Communism in Eastern Europe and the Soviet Union: A Basic Contradiction?*, Basingstoke: Macmillan, 1999.

Ketola, M., *The Nationality Question in the Estonian Evangelical Lutheran Church, 1918–1939*, Helsinki: Finnish Society of Church History, 2000.

King, J., *Budweisers into Czechs and Germans: A Local History of Bohemian Politics, 1848–1948*, Princeton and Oxford: Princeton University Press, 2005.

Klau, S., 'Der Entwurf des neuen Kulturratswahlrechts', *Revalsche Zeitung*, 14 November 1930.

Klimova-Alexander, I., 'Transnational Romani and indigenous non-territorial self-determination claims', in Smith, D. J. and Cordell, K. (eds), *Cultural Autonomy in Contemporary Europe*, London: Routledge, 2008, pp. 59–80.

Koch, H., 'Das Estlandische Deutschtum 1918–1930', *Revalsche Zeitung*, 29 September 1930.

Kogan, A., 'The social democrats and the conflict of nationalities in the Habsburg monarchy', *The Journal of Modern History* 21, 1949, pp. 204–217.

Köll, A.-M., *Peasants on the World Market: Agricultural Experience of Independent Estonia, 1919–1939*, Stockholm: University of Stockholm, 1994.

Koralka, J., 'Nationality representation in Bohemia, Moravia and Austrian Silesia, 1848–1914', in Alderman, G. (ed.), *Governments, Ethnic Groups and Political Representation*, London: Dartmouth, 1993.

Kovacs, M., 'The good, the bad and the ugly: three faces of "dialogue" – the development of Roma politics in Hungary', *Contemporary Politics* 3, 1997, pp. 55–71.

Kovacs, M., 'The political significance of the first national gypsy minority self-government in Hungary', *Contemporary Politics* 6, 2000, pp. 247–262.

Krizsán, A., 'The Hungarian minority protection system: a flexible approach to the adjudication of ethnic claims', *Journal of Ethnic and Migration Studies* 26, 2000, pp. 247–262.

Kurchinskii, M., *Soedinennie shtati Evropy: ekonomicheskie I politicheskie perspektivy etoi idei*, Tartu: Tartu Ülikooli toimetused, 1930.

Kuzio, T., '"Nationalising States" or nation-building? A critical review of the theoretical literature and empirical evidence', *Nations and Nationalism* 7, 2001, pp. 135–154.

Kymlicka, W., 'Nation-building and minority rights: comparing West and East', *Journal of Ethnic and Migration Studies* 26, 2000, pp. 183–212.

Kymlicka, W., *Politics in the Vernacular: Nationalism, Multiculturalism and Citizenship*, Oxford and New York: Oxford University Press, 2001.

Kymlicka, W., *Multicultural Odysseys: Navigating the New International Politics of Diversity*, Oxford and New York: Oxford University Press, 2007.

Kymlicka, W., 'National cultural autonomy and international minority rights norms', in Smith, D. J. and Cordell, K. (eds), *Cultural Autonomy in Contemporary Europe*, London: Routledge, 2008, pp. 43–57.

Kymlicka, W., 'The rise and fall of multiculturalism?: new debates on inclusion and accommodation in diverse societies', in Vertovec, S. and Wessendorf, S. (eds), *The Multiculturalism Backlash*, London and New York: Routledge, 2010, pp. 32–33.

Laurits, K., *Saksa kultuuromavalitsus Eesti Vabariigis 1925–1940*, Tallinn: Rahvusarhiiv, 2008.

Liekis, Š., *A State within a State? Jewish Autonomy in Lithuania 1918–1925*, Vilnius: Versus Aureus, 2003.

Liulevicius, V. G., *War Land on the Eastern Front. Culture, National Identity and German Occupation in World War 1*, Cambridge: Cambridge University Press, 2000.

MacCartney, C. A., *National States and National Minorities*, London: Oxford University Press, 1934.

Madisson, E., *Die nationalen Minderheiten Estlands und ihre Rechte*, Tallinn: Tallinna Eesti Kirjastus-Ühisuse trükikoda, 1926.

Majtény, B., 'Utilitarianism in minority protection? Status laws and international organizations', in Ieda, O (ed.), *Beyond Sovereignty: from Status Law to Transnational Citizenship*, Sapporo: Hokkaido University, 2006, pp. 3–16.

Mann, B., *Die baltischen Länder in der deutschen Kriegszielpublizistik 1914–1918*, Tübingen: J. C. B. Mohr, 1965.

Martin, T., *The Affirmative Action Empire: Nations and Nationalism in the Soviet Union, 1923–39*, Ithaca: Cornell University Press, 2001.

Mendelsohn, E., *The Jews of East-Central Europe between the Two World Wars*, Bloomington: Indiana University Press, 1987.

Mertelsmann, O. with Rahi-Tamm, A., 'Soviet mass violence in Estonia revisited', *Journal of Genocide Research* 11, 2009, pp. 307–322.

Michaelson, R., *Der europäischer Nationalitätenkongress 1925–28. Aufbau, Krise und Konsolidierung*, Frankfurt: Lang, 1984.

Motzkin, L., 'Die Konferenz zum Schutz der jüdischen Minderheitsrechte', *Nation und Staat* 1, 1927.

Müüripeal, E., 'Kultuurautonoomia: Eesti Vabariigi vähemusrahvuste haridus – ja keelepoliitika aastail 1981–1940', Magistritöö [masters dissertation], Tallinn: Tallinna Pedagoogikaülikool, 1999.

Nesemann, F., 'Leo Motzkin (1867–1933). 'Zionist engagement and minority diplomacy', *Central and East European Review* 1, 2007, pp. 32–54.

Newman, A., 'Otto Bauer and contemporary questions of multiculturalism', www.socialistunity.com/?p=1874 (downloaded 23 March 2011).

Nikzentaitis, A., Schreiner, S. and Staliunas, D. (eds), *The Vanished World of Lithuanian Jews*, Amsterdam and New York: Rodopi, 2004.

Nimni, E. J., 'Introduction for the English-reading audience', in Bauer, O., *The Question of Nationalities and Social Democracy*, Minneapolis and London: University of Minnesota Press, 2000.

Nimni, E. J. (ed.), *National Cultural Autonomy and its Contemporary Critics*, London: Routledge, 2005.

Pantenius, H., 'Zur Frage eines Netzes unserer deutschen Schulen', *Revaler Bote*, 21 July 1927.

Pap, A., 'Minority rights and diaspora claims: collision, interdependence and loss of orientation', in Ieda, O. (ed.), *Beyond Sovereignty: from Status Law to Transnational Citizenship*, Sapporo: Hokkaido University, 2006, pp. 243–248.

Pärming, T., 'The Jewish community. Inter-ethnic relations in Estonia, 1918–1940', *Journal of Baltic Studies* 10, 1979, pp. 241–262.

Pearson, R., *National Minorities in Eastern Europe 1848–1944*, London: Macmillan, 1983.

Peters, R., 'Baltic state diplomacy and the League of Nations minorities system', in Hiden J. and Loit A. (eds), *The Baltic in International Relations between the Two World Wars* Stockholm: University of Stockholm, 1988, pp. 281–302.

Petronis, V., *Constructing Lithuania: Ethnic Mapping in Tsarist Russia, ca. 1800–1914*, Stockholm: Stockholm University Press, 2007.

Plakans, A., *The Latvians. A Short History*, Stanford: Hoover Institution Press, 1995.

Prusin, A., *The Lands Between: Conflict in the East European Borderlands, 1870–1992*, Oxford and New York: Oxford University Press, 2010.

Purs, A., 'The price of free lunches: making the frontier Latvian in the inter-war years', *Global Review of Ethnopolitics* 1, 2002, pp. 60–73.

Rajasalu, Ü., 'Russkie v Estonii 1918–1940. Obshchii obzor', in Isakov, S. (ed.), *Russkoe national'noe men'shinstvo v Estonskoi Respublike (1918–1940)*, Tartu: Kripta, 2000, pp. 21–61.

Renner, K. (Springer, R.), *Der Kampf der österreichischen Nationen um den Staat*, Erster Teil: Das nationale Problem als Verfassungs- und Verwaltungsfrage. Leipzig, Wien: Deuticke, 1902.

Renner, K., 'State and nation', in Nimni, E. (ed.), *National Cultural Autonomy and its Contemporary Critics*, London: Routledge, 2005, pp. 13–41.

Robinson, J., 'Die Juden Osteuropas als nationaler Minderheit', *Nation und Staat* 1, 1927.

Roshwald, A., *Ethnic Nationalism and the Fall of Empires: Central Europe, Russia & the Middle East 1914–1923*, London: Routledge, 2001.

Roshwald, A., 'Between balkanisation and banalisation: dilemmas of ethno-cultural diversity', in Smith, D. J. and Cordell, K. (eds), *Cultural Autonomy in Contemporary Europe*, London: Routledge, 2008, pp. 29–42.

Rotbarth, M., 'Grenzrevision und Minderheitenfragen. Zur Funktion des europäischen Minderheiten Kongresses in der Ostpolitik des deutschen Imperialismus', *Studien zur Geschichte der deutsch-polnischen Beziehungen* 6, 1982, pp. 5–30.

Rothschild, J., *East-Central Europe between the Two World Wars*, Seattle: University of Washington Press, 1974.

Rüdiger, W., *Aus dem letzten Kapitel deutsch-baltischer Geschichte in Lettland, 1919–1939*, Hannover: Wülfel, 1955.

Salzborn, S., 'The concept of ethnic minorities. International law and the German-Austrian response', *Behemoth. A Journal on Civilization* 3, 2009, pp. 63–79.

Scheuermann, M., *Minderheitenschutz contra Konfliktverhütung: Die Minderheitenpolitik des Völkerbundes in den zwanziger Jahren*, Marburg: Johann Gottfried Herder-Institut, 2000.

Schiemann, P., 'Schlechte Waffen', *Rigasche Rundschau*, 1 January 1907.

Schiemann, P., 'Ich warne', *Rigasche Rundschau*, 12 March 1920.

Schiemann, P., 'Die nationalen Minderheiten in Lettland', *Zeitschrift für Politik* 14, 1925, pp. 276–281.

Schiemann, P., 'Minoritätenschutz und Nationalitätenrecht', *Rigasche Rundschau*, 20 February 1926.

Schiemann, P., 'Die Minderheiten. P. Schiemann über die Ergebnisse des Genfer-Kongresses', *Rigascher Rundschau*, 4 September 1926.

Schiemann, P., 'Die vereitelte Minderheitenfront', *Rigasche Rundschau*, 30 October 1926.

Schiemann, P., 'Streitfragen des Nationalitätenkongresses', *Rigasche Rundschau*, 1 October 1927.

Schiemann, P., 'Die Spaltung im Nationalitätenkongress', *Nation und Staat* 1, 1928, pp. 158–170.

Schiemann, P., 'Heilige Rechte', *Rigasche Rundschau*, 22 December 1928.

Schiemann, P., 'Die kollektivistische Gefahr', *Rigasche Rundschau*, 18 January 1930.

Schiemann, P., 'Coudenhove und Rohan', *Nation und Staat* 10/11, 1930, pp. 630–636.

Schiemann, P., 'Das Herr in Lettland', *Rigasche Rundschau*, 1 August 1931.

Schiemann, P., 'Pessimismus und Optimismus. Rede von Dr. P. Schiemann, gehalten auf dem Nationalitätenkongress in Genf', *Rigasche Rundschau*, 5 September 1931.

Schiemann, P., 'Nationalitäten-kongress', *Rigasche Rundschau*, 12 September 1931.

Schiemann, P., 'Einheitskultur', *Rigasche Rundschau*, 9 January 1932.

Schiemann, P., 'Hüben und Drüben', *Rigasche Rundschau*, 30 January 1932.

Schiemann, P., *'Die neue nationalistische Welle'*. The original manuscript for this is in the Schiemann Nachlass, Baltijas Centrale Biblioteka, Riga. Drei Manuskripte 1932–1939, no. 1. For an English-language translation, see *Central and East European Review*, 1, 2007 http://spaces.brad.ac.uk:8080/display/ssishistoryjournal (downloaded on 6 July 2010).

Schiemann, P., 'Dissimilation und Nationalitätenrechte' Dokumente aus dem politischen Nachlass von Hans Otto Roth 1919–1951. Nr 232 pp. 420–424. Draft text of speech that Schiemann had intended to deliver at the Bern meeting of the Nationalities Congress on 16–19 September 1933. Kindly made available to the authors by Dr Hildrun Glass.

Schiemann, P., 'Zielsetzung der Minderheiten', *Der Deutsche in Polen*, 28 June 1936.

Schiemann, P., 'Die Umsiedlung 1939 und die europäischer Minderheitenpolitik', unpublished manuscript written in Riga in spring 1940.

Schiemann, P., *Zwischen zwei Zeitaltern. Erinnerungen 1903–1919*, Lüneburg: Nordland-Druck, 1979.

Scholsem, J.-C., 'Personal autonomy through the "communities system": does the example of Belgium suggest that forms of non-territorial autonomy can make a difference in terms of minority participation?" in Venice Commission, *The Participation of Minorities in Public Life*, Collection science and technique of democracy, Number 45, Strasbourg: Council of Europe Publishing, 2008, pp. 101–118.

Schöpflin, G., *Nations, Identity, Power: The New Politics of Europe*, London: Hurst, 2000.

Schot, B., *Stresemann, der deutsche Osten und der Völkerbund*, Wiesbaden: Zabern, 1984.

Schot, B., *Nation oder Staat. Deutschland und der Minderheitenschutz*, Marburg: Johann-Gottfried Herder Institut, 1988.

Sitzungsbericht des Kongresses der Organisierten Nationalen Gruppen in den Staaten Europas, Genf, 25 bis 27 August 1926, Vienna and Leipzig: Willhelm Braumüller, 1927 onwards.

Sitzungsbericht des Kongresses der Organisierten Nationalen Gruppen in den Staaten Europas, Bern, 16 bis 18. September 1933, Vienna and Leipzig: Willhelm Braumüller, 1934.

Smith, D. J., 'Retracing Estonia's Russians: Mikhail Kurchinskii and interwar cultural autonomy', *Nationalities Papers* 27, 1999, pp. 455–474.

Smith, D. J., 'Cultural autonomy in Estonia. A relevant paradigm for the post-Soviet era?', ESRC 'One Europe or Several?' working paper 19/01, 2001.

Smith D. J. (ed.), *The Baltic States and their Region: New Europe or Old?*, Amsterdam and New York: Rodopi, 2005.

Smith, D. J. and Cordell, K. (eds), *Cultural Autonomy in Contemporary Europe*, London: Routledge, 2008.

Smith, G. (ed.), *The Nationalities Question in the Post-Soviet States*, London: Longman, 1996.

Smith, G., Law, V., Wilson, A., Bohr, A. and Allworth, E., *Nation-Building in the Post-Soviet Borderlands. The Politics of National Identities*, Cambridge: Cambridge University Press, 1998.

Smith, J., *The Bolsheviks and the National Question 1917–23*, London: Macmillan, 1999.

Bibliography 157

Springer, R. (pseudonym of Renner, K.), *Grundlagen und Entwicklungsziele der österreichisch-ungarischen Monarchie*, Vienna: 1906, p. 208.

Stalin, J. V., *Works*, vol. 2, Moscow: Foreign Languages Publishing House, 1954.

Stalin, J. V., 'Marxism and the national question', in Stalin, J. V., *Works*, vol. 2, Moscow: Foreign Languages Publishing House, 1954, pp. 303–313.

Staliunas, D., *Making Russians: Meaning and Practice of Russification in Lithuania and Belarus after 1863*, Amsterdam and New York: Rodopi, 2007.

Šteimanis, J., *History of Latvian Jews*, New York: Columbia University Press, 2002.

Stresemann, G., 'Die Minderheitenfrage als Friedensproblem', *Kölnische Volkszeitung. Sonderbeilage*, 1 August 1929.

Suny, R. G. and Martin, T. (eds), *A State of Nations: Empire and Nation Making in the Age of Lenin and Stalin*, Oxford: Oxford University Press, 2001.

Tauber, J., ' "No allies". The Lithuanian *Taryba* and the national minorities 1916–1918', *Journal of Baltic Studies* 38, 2007, pp. 433–444.

Tauber, J. and Tuchtenhagen, R., *Vilnius. Kleine Geschichte der Stadt*, Cologne, Weimar, Vienna: Böhlau, 2008.

Thaden, E. (ed.), *Russification in the Baltic Provinces and Finland 1855–1914*, Princeton: Princeton University Press, 1981.

Tolz, V., *Russia: Inventing the Nation*, London: Arnold, 2001.

Van der Stoel, M., *Peace and Stability through Human and Minority Rights: Speeches by the OSCE High Commissioner on National Minorities*, Baden Baden: Nomos Verlagsgesellschaft, 1999.

Vardys, V. S. and Misiunas, R. J. (eds), *The Baltic States in Peace and War 1917–1945*, Philadelphia and London: The Pennsylvania State University Press, 1978.

Venice Commission, *The Participation of Minorities in Public Life*. Collection science and technique of democracy, Number 45, Strasbourg: Council of Europe Publishing, 2008.

Verschik, A., 'The Yiddish language in Estonia: past and present', *Journal of Baltic Studies* 30, 1999, pp. 117–127.

Vertovec, S. and Wessendorf, S. (eds), *The Multiculturalism Backlash*, London and New York: Routledge, 2010.

Vertovec, S. and Wessendorf, S., 'Introduction: assessing the backlash against multiculturalism in Europe', in Vertovec, S. and Wessendorf, S. (eds), *The Multiculturalism Backlash*, London and New York: Routledge, 2010.

Volkmann, H. E., *Die deutsche Baltikumpolitik zwischen Brest-Litovsk und Compiègne*, Cologne: Böhlau, 1970.

Volkovs, V. *Krievi Latvijā*, Rīga: Latvijas Zinātņu akadēmijas Filozofijas un socioloģijas institūta Etnisko pētījumu centrs, 1996.

von Hehn, J., *Die Umsiedlung der baltischen Deutschen – das letzte Kapitel baltisch-deutscher Geschichte*, Marburg/Lahn: Herder-Institut, 1982.

von Hehn, J., von Rimscha, H. and Weiss, H. (eds), *Von den baltischen Provinzen zu den baltischen Staaten: Beiträge zur Entstehungsgeschichte der Republiken Estland und Lettland*, Marburg: Johan Gottfried Herder Institut, 1977.

von Pistohlkors, G., 'Führende Schicht oder nationale Minderheit', *Zeitschrift für Ostforschung* 21, 1972, pp. 601–618.

von Rauch, G., *The Baltic States. The Years of Independence 1917–1940*, London: Hurst, 1995.

Wachtsmuth, W., *Von deutscher Arbeit in Lettland 1918–1934. Ein Tätigskeitbericht. Materialen zur Geschichte des baltischen Deutschtums. Vol. 1: die deutschbaltische Volksgemeinschaft in Lettland 1923–1934*, Cologne: Comel Verlag, 1951.

Wachtsmuth, W., *Von deutscher Arbeit in Lettland 1918–1934. Ein Tätigskeitbericht. Materialen zur Geschichte des baltischen Deutschtums. Vol. 2: die autonome deutsche Schule in Lettland 1920–1934*, Cologne: Comel Verlag, 1952.

Wachtsmuth, W., *Von deutscher Arbeit in Lettland 1918–1934. Ein Tätigskeitbericht. Materialen zur Geschichte des baltischen Deutschtums. Vol. 3: das politische Gesicht der deutschen Volksgruppe in Lettland in der parlamentarische Period 1918–1933*, Cologne: Comel Verlag, 1953.

Webb, A., *The Routledge Companion to Central and Eastern Europe since 1919*, London: Routledge, 2008.

Index

Taylor & Francis

eBooks

FOR LIBRARIES

ORDER YOUR FREE 30 DAY INSTITUTIONAL TRIAL TODAY!

Over 23,000 eBook titles in the Humanities, Social Sciences, STM and Law from some of the world's leading imprints.

Choose from a range of subject packages or create your own!

Benefits for **you**

- ▶ Free MARC records
- ▶ COUNTER-compliant usage statistics
- ▶ Flexible purchase and pricing options

Benefits for your **user**

- ▶ Off-site, anytime access via Athens or referring URL
- ▶ Print or copy pages or chapters
- ▶ Full content search
- ▶ Bookmark, highlight and annotate text
- ▶ Access to thousands of pages of quality research at the click of a button

For more information, pricing enquiries or to order a free trial, contact your local online sales team.

UK and Rest of World: **online.sales@tandf.co.uk**

US, Canada and Latin America:
e-reference@taylorandfrancis.com

www.ebooksubscriptions.com

ALPSP Award for BEST eBOOK PUBLISHER 2009 Finalist

Taylor & Francis **eBooks**
Taylor & Francis Group

A flexible and dynamic resource for teaching, learning and research.